1835 CHEROKEE VALUATIONS

ABSTRACTED
BY
Marjorie J. Lowe

HERITAGE BOOKS
2012

HERITAGE BOOKS
AN IMPRINT OF HERITAGE BOOKS, INC.

Books, CDs, and more—Worldwide

For our listing of thousands of titles see our website
at
www.HeritageBooks.com

Published 2012 by
HERITAGE BOOKS, INC.
Publishing Division
100 Railroad Ave. #104
Westminster, Maryland 21157

Copyright © 2012 Marjorie J. Lowe

All rights reserved. No part of this book may be reproduced or transmitted in any form or by any means, electronic or mechanical, including photocopying, recording or by any information storage and retrieval system without written permission from the author, except for the inclusion of brief quotations in a review.

International Standard Book Numbers
Paperbound: 978-0-7884-5450-9
Clothbound: 978-0-7884-9244-0

TABLE OF CONTENTS

Introduction	p. i
Valuations	p. 1
Bibliography	p. 84
Index	p. 85

Dedication

Honoring my Grandchildren's Heritage:

Hunter, Cameron and Brynne Elizabeth Herzfeld

INTRODUCTION

From the time of the Louisiana Purchase in 1804, plans were being made as to how to peacefully remove the five tribes residing in the southeastern U.S. to west of the Mississippi. Various rolls and census records were taken of individual heads of households to use for a persuasive means to succeed in signing treaties to accomplish this task. In the case of the Cherokee Tribe, once the Treaty of New Echota was signed in 1835, the federal government developed a means of compensating those who would be removed. They evaluated the improvements on the land for what would be lost by the forced removal to the west.

On February 28th, 1839, U.S. Senate, 25th Congress, 3rd Session Report from the Secretary of War was read and ordered to be printed. This constitutes the first part of this work which contains the names of persons employed, their duties, their compensation and the funds furnished to complete the ordered tasks. Some of those employed had Cherokee wives, others were mixed-blood Cherokees, but most were non-Cherokee.

The second section listed the Cherokee heads of households and the amount of each evaluation. The index also notes those Cherokee citizens who were also enumerated on the Cherokee 1835 U.S. Federal Census.

Thanks goes to Thomas Mooney, Cherokee Heritage Center, Archivist; Jack D. Baker, Cherokee Tribal Councilor, Historian and Genealogist; and to the late Dr. Stan Hoig, Author, Professor and Oklahoma Inductee of the Historian's Hall of Fame, for their guidance, advice and encouragement.

Marjorie J. Lowe
Houston, TX

Statement of all persons, other than officers of the army, employed under the authority of the United States, in carrying into effect the provisions of the treaty with the Cherokee Indians, of December 29, 1835, with the duty each was expected to perform, the rate of compensation promised to each, and by whom the appointments were made, & c.

Names	Duties	Appointed Date.	Sum Paid.	Appointed by Whom	Remarks
Wilson Lumpkin	Commissioner	7/7/1836	$8 per Day.	President & Senate	Resigned
John Kennedy	Do.	10/25/1836	Do.	Do.	
Thomas W. Wilson	Do.	10/16/1837	Do.	Do.	
James Liddell	Do.	12/22/1837	Do.	Do.	Appointed in place of Gov. Lumpkin, resigned. Resigned 2/16/1838.
William R. Jackson	Secretary to Commish.	7/12/1836	$5 per Day.	Sec. Of War.	11/30/1837 -3/9/1838, Performed duties as Sec. Pro Tem, Col. Jackson being Absent without leave.
John C. Mullay	Do.	3/9/1838	Do.	Do.	
Benjamin f. Currey	Supt. Of Emigration	5/23, 1836	$2,000	President	Died Dec. 16, 1836.
Nathaniel Smith	Do.	1/3/1837	$2,000	Do.	Appointed in place of Major Currey, deceased. Service Terminated by order of Dept.
John S. Young	Asst. Supt. Of Emigration.	1/23/1837	$4 per Day	Supt of Emigration	Discontinued
William N. Bishop	Valuing Indian Improvements.	8/17/1837	Do.	Do.	Discont'd. Appointment temp.
David Caldwell	Do.	8/16/1836	Do.	Do.	Do.
Philip Hemphill	Do.	8/30/1836	Do.	Do.	Do.
N. L. Hutchins	Do.	9/5/1836	Do.	Do.	Do.
N. S. Jarrett					Discont'd. Appointment Temp.

Statement of all persons, other than officers of the army, employed under the authority of the United States, in carrying into effect the provisions of the treaty with the Cherokee Indians, of December 29, 1835, with the duty each was expected to perform, the rate of compensation promised to each, and by whom the appointments were made, & c.

Names	Duties	Appointed Date.	Sum Paid.	Appointed by Whom	Remarks
Wilson Lumpkin	Commissioner	7/7/1836	$3 per Day.	President & Senate	Resigned
John Kennedy	Do.	10/25/1836	Do.	Do.	
Thomas W. Wilson	Do.	10/16/1837	Do.	Do.	
James Liddell	Do.	12/22/1837	Do.	Do.	
William R. Jackson	Secretary to Commish.	7/12/1836	$5 per Day.	Sec. Of War.	Appointed in place of Gov. Lumpkin, resigned. Resigned 2/16/1838.
John C. Mullay	Do.	3/9/1838	Do.	Do.	11/30/1837 -3/9/1838, Performed duties as Sec. Pro Tem, Col. Jackson being Absent without leave.
Benjamin f. Currey	Supt. Of Emigration	5/23, 1836	$2,000	President	Died Dec. 16, 1836.
Nathaniel Smith	Do.	1/3/1837	$2,000	Do.	Appointed in place of Major Currey, deceased. Service Terminated by order of Dept.
John S. Young	Asst. Supt. Of Emigration.	1/23/1837	$4 per Day	Supt of Emigration	Discontinued
William N. Bishop	Valuing Indian Improvements.	8/17/1837	Do.	Do.	Discont'd. Appointment temp.
David Caldwell	Do.	8/16/1836	Do.	Do.	Do. Do.
Philip Hemphill	Do.	8/30/1836	Do.	Do.	Do. Do.
N. L. Hutchins	Do.	9/5/1836	Do.	Do.	Do. Do.
N. S. Jarrett					Discont'd. Appointment Temp.

Name	Role	Date	Pay	Position	Notes
James Liddell	Do.	8/30/1836	Do.	Do.	Reappointed 11/27/1837, by the Commissioners, then discont'd.
Joseph McMillan	Do.	8/22/1836	Do.	Do.	Discont'd. Appoint Temp.
Stephen Mays	Do.	8/17/1836	Do.	Do.	Discontinued.
George S. Massey	Do.	9/21/1836	Do.	Do.	Discont'd. Appoint. Temp.
Andrew Moore	Do.	9/22/1836	Do.	Do.	Do. Do.
David Ricketts	Do.	9/23/1836	Do.	Do.	Do. Do.
Jackson Smith	Do.	8/16/1836	Do.	Do.	Do. Do.
Josiah Shaw	Do.	9/5/1836	Do.	Do.	Resigned 11/24/1837.
William Welch	Do.	8/24/1836	Do.	Do.	Discontinued.
John S. Young	Do.	8/11/1836	Do.	Do.	Do.
Joel Yancy	Do.	8/20/1836	Do.	Do.	Do.
Rezin Rwlings	Do.	9/19/1836	Do.	Do.	Do.
L. A. Kincannon	Do.	8/25/1837	Do.	Commissioners.	Employed but a "few days."
John S. Hare	Do.	11/21/1837	Do.	Supt. Of Emigr.	Discont'd.
J. R. Love	Do.	11/28/1837	Do.	Commissioners	Discont'd
Preston Starrett	Conducting & Enrolling Emig.	7/1/1837	Do.	Supt. Of Emgr.	Discont'd. 11/25/1837. Reappointed 2/19/1838, Discont'd again 3/13.
Aaron Haynes	Do.	9/21/1837	Do.	Do.	Discont'd 12/3/1827.
G.S. Massey	Do.	9/11/1837	Do.	Do.	Discont'd.
C.D. Terhun	Do.	9/11/1837	Do.	Do.	Discont'd. 11/30/1837.
Henry McKay	Do.	9/11/1837	Do.	Do.	Discont'd 12/1/1837.
Nicholas Byers	Do.	10/30/1837	Do.	Do.	Discontin'd 11/22/1837.
J.S. Young	Do.	1/23/1837	Do.	Do.	Discontin'd.
B.B. Cannon	Do.	10/13/1837	Do.	Do.	Discontin'd.
Josiah Shaw	Do.	2/6/1838	$4 per Day.	Do.	Discontin'd 5/7/1838.

T.C. Hindman	Do.	1/15/1838	Discontin'd 4/11/1838.
J.F. Beavers	Do.	1/15/1838	Discontin'd 3/16/1838
J.W. Webb	Do.	1/15/1838	Discontin'd.
Peter Reagan	Do.	2/25/1838	Discontin'd 4/9/1838.
Moses Daniel	Do.	2/25/1838	Discontin'd 3/24/1838.
E.S. Currey	Do.	1/24/1838	Discontin'd 3/211838. He acted as assist. Conductor, for which he received $3 per day.
A.S. Lanair	Do.	June, 1838	Discontin'd.
L.A. Kincannon	Do.	June, 1838	Discontin'd.
Rider Fields	Assist. Supt.	7/23/1837	Discontin'd.
A.R. Barclay	Do.	7/25/1837	Discontin'd.
Milo Smith	Do.	1/25/1837	Discontin'd.
D.S. Walker	Do.	June, 1838	Discontin'd.
A. Cox	Do.	June, 1838	Discontin'd.
Harlin	Do.	June, 1838	Discontin'd.
B.B. Cannon	Collected Indians Prior to Removal.	2/7/1837	$2.50 per Day. Discontin'd 10/12/1837. Re-Appointed 1/1/1838, Discontin'd Again 3/24/1838.
E. S. Currey	Do.	1/25/1827	Discontin'd 10/12/1837.
J.W. Webb	Do.	8/22/1837	Discontin'd 12/16/1837.
Joseph McCulley	Do.	2/6/1837	Discontin'd 11/19/1837. Re-Appointed 2/20/1838, disontinu'd Again 3/21/1838.
L.A. Kincannon	Do.	3/8/1837	Discontin'd.
Rezin Rawlings	Do.	9/8/1837	Discontin'd 4/5/1838.
James Landerdale	Do.	9/15/1837	Discontin'd 11/19/1836.
T.C. Hindman	Do.	10/5/1837	Discontin'd 1/1/1838.
G.S. Massey	Do.	1/1/1837	Discontin'd 3/5/1837.
Stephen Hempstead	Do.	12/16/1837	Discontin'd.

Name	Role	Date	Pay	Supervisor	Notes
Jonathn Carr	Do.	1/20/1838	Do.	Do.	Discontin'd 4/30/1838.
Abraham Barb	Do.	2/3/1838	Do.	Do.	Discontin'd 2/20/1838.
J. McCrary	Do.	2/10/1838	Do.	Do.	Discontin'd 3/16/1838.
R.M. Hook	Do.	1/1/1838	Do.	Do.	Discontin'd.
Allen Kennedy	Do.	2/10/1838	Do.	Do.	Discontin'd 3/26/1838.
E.H. Boyd	Do.	10/23/1837	Do	Do.	Discontin'd 11/16/1837. Re-Appointed 2/7/1838, discontin'd 3/21/1838, again.
O. G. Parry	Do.	2/16/1838	Do.	Do.	Discontin'd.
W. Easley	Do.	June, 1838	Do.	Do.	Discontin'd.
W. Smith	Do.	June, 1838	Do.	Do.	Discontin'd
T.J. Kelley	Do.	June, 1838	Do.	Do.	Discontin'd
J. Garrett	Do.	June, 1838	Do.	Do.	Discontin'd.
C. Lillybridge	Physician	10/10/1836	$5 per Day.	Do.	Discontin'd. Portion of time Received $6 per day.
J. W. Lide	Directing	2/18/1837	$6 per Day.	Emigr. Supt.	Discontin'd/
G.S. Townsend	Do.	5/2/1837	$5 per Day.	Sec. Of War	Discontin'd.
James Hunter	Do.	2/6/1837	Do.	Emigr. Supt.	Discontin'd. Portion of time Received 43.50 per day.
A.M. Folger	Do	2/22/1837	Do.	Do.	Discontin'd.
Cottle	Do	June, 1838	Do.	Do.	Discontin'd.
J.W. Netherland	Do.	June, 1838	Do.	Do.	Discontin'd.
R.H. hodsden	Do.	9/13/1837	Do.	Do.	Discontin'd.
E.H. Eiffert	Issuing Rations.	9/13/1837	$1 Per Day.	Do.	Discontin'd. 11/17/1837.
C. Milligan	Do.	8/1/1837	Do.	Do.	Discontin'd 11/8/1837.
George Orr	Do.	2/6/1837	Do.	Do.	Discontin'd 2/28/1837.
J.M. Bruce	Do.	2/6/1837	$2 ½ per Day.	Do.	Discontin'd 3/5/1937.
G.S. Denton	Do.	3/8/1837	Do.	Do.	Discontin'd 12/12/1837.
N.B. Darmerburg	Do.	7/9/1838	$66 per mon.	Capt. J.R. Stephenson	Issuing agent west of Misssissippi.

Name	Position	Date	Pay	Reporting to	Status
Joel Crittenden	Disbursing Agent	10/7/1837	$5 per day.	Sec. Of War	Discontin'd.
V. Van Antwerp	Do.	10/11/1837	Do.	Do.	Resigned.
H.W. Hargrove	Office Clerk for Commissioners.	------	$3 per day.	Commissioners	Discontin'd.
George W. Currey	Do.	3/17/1837	$5 per day.	Do.	Relieved 10/28/1837.
J.L. Sparks	Do.	-	$3 per day.	Do.	Discontin'd.
John M. Gifford	Do.	-	Do.	Do.	Discontin'd.
Edward Schrivener	Do.	-	Do.	Do.	Discontin'd.
W.W. Laddell	Do.	-	Do.	Do.	Discontin'd.
James K. Love	Do.	-	Do.	Do.	Discontin'd.
C.K. Gillispie	Do.	-	Do.	Do.	Discontin'd.
John W. Mayo	Do.	-	Do.	Do.	Discontin'd.
T.H. McCallie	Do.	-	Do.	Do.	Discontin'd.
H.B. Gaither	Do.	-	Do.	Do.	Discontin'd
J.W.H. Dawson	Do.	-	Do.	Do.	Discontin'd
D.S. Bell	Do.	-	Do.	Do.	Discontin'd.
S.S. McGuire	Do.	-	Do.	Do.	Discontin'd.
J.N. Hetzell	Office Clerk For Supt.	2/1/1837.	Do.	Supt. Of Emigr.	Discontin'd.
Spencer Jarnigan	Do.	2/1/1837	Do.	Do.	Discontin'd.
John C. Mulloy	Disbursing Clerk	10/1/1837	$5 per day	Do.	Discontin'd 11/30/1837.
Johnson Alberd	Interpreter*	9/6/1836	$2 ½ per day.	Do.	Discontin'd.
Harry Crittenden	Do.	9/2/1836	Do.	Do.	Discontin'd.
J. A. Foreman	Do.	8/21/1836	Do.	Do.	Discontin'd.
William Foreman	Do.	8/21/1836	Do.	Do.	Discontin'd.
Fiesca Fields	Do.	8/25/1836	Do.	Do.	Discontin'd.
Michael Gormley	Do.	8/25/1836	Do.	Do.	Discontin'd. Reappointed 1/15/1838, discontin'd 2/10/1838 again.
Ellis S. Harlan	Do.	12/9/1835	$500 per an.	Do.	Discontin'd.

Name	Role	Date	Pay		Status
William Lasley	Do.	9/24/1836		Do.	Discontin'd.
Andrew Ross	Do.	9/1/19/1836		Do.	Discontin'd.
Preston Starrett	Interpreter	6/10/1836		Supt. of Emig.	Discontin'd.
John Watie	Do.	8/21/1836		Do.	Discontin'd.
David Foreman	Do.	2/21/1837		Do.	Discontin'd.
D.J. Bell	Do.	2/21/1837		Do.	Discontin'd. 11/4/1837. Re-appointed 2/20/1838, Discontin'd 3/24/38, again.
Mark Tiger	Do.	2/24/1837	$2 ½ per day.	Do.	Discontin'd. Reappointed 9/5/1837, discontin'd again 11/16/1837.
William H. Foreman	Do.	9/6/1837	Do.	Do.	Discontin'd 10/13/1837.
Ezekiel Byers	Do.	9/23/1837	Do.	Do.	Discontin'd 11/21/1837.
James Bigby	Do.	9/23/1837	Do.	Do.	Discontin'd 11/19/1837, Re-Appointed 1/14/1838, again
Thomas Jones	Do.	9/25/1837	Do.	Do.	Discontin'd.
Alexander McCoy	Do.	1/25/1837	Do.	Do.	Discontin'd.
Charles Reese	Do.	3/3/1837	Do.	Do.	Discontin'd. Reappointed 8/24/1837, discontin'd again.
Elijah Hicks	Do.	3/3/1837	Do.	Do.	Discontin'd.
George Candy	Do.	4/2/1837	Do.	Do.	Discontin'd.
Johnston Fields	Do.	4/2/1837	Do.	Do.	Discontin'd.
Leonard Hicks	Do.	4/2/1837	Do.	Do.	Discontin'd.
C.W. Hicks	Do.	4/2/1837	Do.	Do.	Discontin'd.
William Reese	Do.	4/2/1837	Do.	Do.	Discontin'd.
William Steele	Do.	7/23/1837	Do.	Do.	Discontin'd.
J.A. Bell	Do.	8/1/1837	Do.	Do.	Discontin'd.
B.W. Wisner	Do.	12/18/1837	Do.	Do.	Discontin'd.
Jay Hicks	Do.	2/5/1838	Do.	Do.	Discontin'd.

Name	Role	Date	Pay	Status
Daniel D. Spencer	Do.	10/28/1837	Do.	Discontin'd 1/21/1837.
Samuel Wisner	Do.	1/1/1838	Do.	Discontin'd 4/11/1838.
William Huss	Do.	10/28/1837	Do.	Discontin'd 12/23/1837, Re-appointed 2/21 and Discontin'd 3/7/1838.
Richard Guess	Do.	1/17/1838	Do.	Discontin'd 3/16/1838.
John Kell	Do.	2/26/1838	Do.	Discontin'd 3/27/1838.
Robertson Brown, Jr.	Do.	1/17/1838	Do.	Discontin'e 3/27/1838.
David Steiner, Jr.	Do.	2/7/1838	Do.	Discontin'd 3/26/1838.
Nelson Chamberlain	Do.	9/29/1837	Do.	Discontin'd 3/21/1838.
Nelson Ore	Do.	2/1/1838	Do.	Discontin'd.
William P. Davis	Do.	11/9/1837	Do.	Discontin'd 3/27/1838.
Richard Ratcliff, Jr.	Do.	9/23/1837	Do.	Discontin'd 2/1/1838.
J.P. Thompson	Do.	9/12/1837	Do.	Discontin'd 11/21/1837.
Jesse Hicks	Do.	June, 1838	Do.	Discontin'd.
J. McPherson	Do.	June, 1838	Do.	Discontin'd.*
Robertson Brown	Do.	June, 1838	Do.	Discontin'd.
Denis Wolf	Do.	June, 1838	Do.	Discontin'd.
John Drew	Do.	June, 1838	Do.	Discontin'd.
E.S. Harlin	Do.	------	Commissioners.	Discontin'd.
D.J. Bell	Do	------	Do.	Discontin'd.
Josiah Reese	Do.	11/28/1837	Do	Discontin'd.
Betsy Wooward	Do.	------	Do.	Discontin'd.
Lewis Griffin	Do.	------	Do.	Discontin'd.
J.M.D. Reese	Do.	------	Do.	Discontin'd.
Henry Smith	Do.	11/30/1837	Do.	Discontin'd.
Jourdon Smith	Receiving & storing Provisions.	2/23/1837	$2½ & $3 per day. Supt. of Emig.	Discontin'd 4/15/1837.
William Chester	Wagon Master	2/2/1837	$2½ per day.	Do.	Discontin'd 2/6/1837.
J. Morris	Boat Steerer	3/3/1837	$1½ per day.	Dol.	Discontin'd 3/7/1837.

G.S. Denton		Do.	2/28/1827	Do.	Discontin'd 3/7/1837.
C. Johnson		Do.	3/4/1837	Do.	Discontin'd 3/7/1837.
Mary Moore	Hospital Matron		5/1/1837	$1 per day.	Discontin'd.
E. Downing		Do.	2/22/1837	Do.	Discontin'd.
Olley Lassly		Do.	10/13/1837	Do.	Discontin'd.
R.A. Ramsey	Wagon Master		June, 1838	$2 ½ per day.	Discontin'd.
Betsy Woodward	Hospital Matron and interpreter.		June, 1838	Do.	Discontin'd.
Susan Hair		Do.	June, 1838	Do.	Discontin'd.

* The above list embraces the interpreters to the commissioners, the valuing, collecting, enrolling, conducting, and disbursing agents, the physicians, &c. Office of Indian Affairs, Feb. 1839.

Statement showing the species of funds paid to agents to carry into effect the provisions of the treaty of Dec. 29, 1835, &c.

Date of Payment	In Whose Favor	Warrant Amount	Where Payable	Draft Amount	Remarks
7/16/1836	William D. Lewis	$250,000	Girard Bank, Philadelphia	$ 50,000	
			Union Bank of Maryland	50,000	
			Movamensing Bank, Philadelphia	50,000	
			Manhattan Bank, New York	50,000	
			Mechanics' Bank, New York	50,000	
7/25/1836	J.D. Beers	70,626.66	Mechanics' Bank, New York	50,000	
7/29/1836	W.H. Haywood	309,060.09	Mechanics' Bank, New York	70,625.65	
8/1/1836	William D. Lewis	93,973.31	Bank of America, New York	309,060.09	
8/29/1836	Gen. J.E. Wool	10,000	Mechanics' Bank, New York	93,973.34	
9/30/1836	Gen. J.E. Wool	10,000	Bank of Metropolis, Washington	10,000	
			Planter's Bank, Tennessee	5,000	
			Bank of America, New York	5,000	

x

Date	Name	Amount	Bank	Amount
10/22/1836	P. Minus	$ 4,000	Planters' Bank, Tennessee	$ 4,000
10/28/1836	P. Minus	8,505	Bank of Augusta, Georgia	8,505
11/3/1836	P. Minus	50,000	Planters' Bank, Tennessee	50,000
11/5/1836	P. Minus	200,000	Planters' Bank, Tennessee	200,000
12/7/1836	Joseph White	880	Mechanics' Bank, New York	880
12/29/1836	P. Minus	250,000	Planter' Bank, Augusta, GA	250,000
2/15/1837	S.B. Everitt	80.60	Bank of North Carolina	80.60
2/16/1837	J. Brown	20,000	Union Bank, New Orleans	20,000
2/16/1837	Buckingham & Huntington	15,159.81	Mechanics Bank, New York	15,159.81
2/25/1836	S.C. Owens	332.00	Girard Bank, Philadelphia	332.00
3/2/1837	J. McCoy	500.00	Bank of Metropolis, Washington	500.00
3/6/1837	J.C. Reynolds	25,000	Manhattan Company, Nw York	25,000
3/6/1837	George Thomas	400.00	Bank of Metropolis, Washington	400.00
3/21/1837	Cashier/Bank of Augusta	200,000	Bank of Augusta, Georgia	200,000
3/29/1837	Cashier/Planter's Branch	100,000	Planter's Bank, Nashville	100,000
3/29/1837	George Thomas	25,000	Bank of Metropolis, Washington	25,000
3/29/1837	R.D.C. Collins	150,000	Agricultural Bank, Natchez	150,000
7/3/1837	Joseph Hook, Jr.	150,000	Branch Bank/IN, Lawrenceburg	116,991.00
			Savings Institution, Louisville	8,009.00
			Receiver, Marietta, OH	10,000.00
			Receiver, Cincinnati, OH	5,000.00
			Receiver, Shawneetown, IN	10,000.00
7/6/1837	Joseph Hook, Jr.	5,000	Union Bank, Baltimore	5,000.00
7/20/1837	J.P. Simenton	200,000	Bank of Charleston, SC	40,609.00
			Planters' & Mechanics' Bank, SC	39,400.00
			Bank of Augusta, GA	37,000
			Planter's Bank, GA	30,000
			Ins. Bank, Columbus, GA	5,035
			Receiver, Montgomery, Alabama	22,965
			Augusta, Mississippi	25,000

Date	Name	Amount	Institution	Amount
8/11/1837	J.C. Reynolds	40,000	Savings Institution, Louisville	$ 2,500
			Receiver, Shawneetown, IL	8,000
10/9/1837	J. Crittenden	8,000	Receiver, Kaskaskia, IL	12,000
10/24/1837	V. Van Antwerp	10,000	Bank of KY, Louisville	8,000
11/8/1837	Cashier Bank of Washington	50,000	Treasury notes	10,000
			Receiver, Lima, OH	40,000
12/19/1837	J.P. Simonton	100,000	Receiver, Chillicothe, OH	10,000
11/21/1837	L.G. De Russy	150,000	Treasury notes	100,000
			Receiver, Washington, AR	6,173
			Receiver, Jeffersonville,	19,320
			Bank of IL	10,507
12/12/1837	W. Coston	1,500	Savings Institution, Louisville	114,000
12/16/1837	V. Van Antwerp	80,000	Treasury Notes	1,500
			Receiver, Huntsville, AL	15,000
			Receiver, Shawneetown	11,000
			Receiver, Cincinnati	7,000
			Receiver, Fort Wayne	10,000
			Northern bank of KY	5,000
			Bank of Illinois	2,000
3/24/1838	Isaac McCoy	1904.24	Savings Institution, Louisville	30,000
			Receiver, Lexington	7,000
			Commercial Bank, Cincinnati	154.24
3/24/1838	R T. Hanks	475.00	Union Bank, TN	475.00
5/4/1838	V.P. Van Antwerp	257.60	Savings Institution, Louisville	257.60
6/2/1838	J.P. Simonton	100,000	Treasury Notes	100,000
6/23/1838	John Page	100,000	Bank of Manhattan, New York	30,000
			Treasury Notes	70,000
6/29/1838	John Page	100,000	Bank of American, New York	50,000

Date	Name	Amount	Description	Amount	Status
7/10/1838	J.L. Williams		Treasury Notes	50,000	
7/25/1838	J.P. Simonton	210	Manhattan Company, New York	210	
8/29/1838	John Page	100,000	Treasury Notes	100,000	
		200,000	Treasury Notes	50,000	
			Bank of America, New York	64,000	
			Bank of United States of PA	86,000	
9/13/1838	John Page	11,296.55	Bank of U.S. of PA, Nashville	11,296.55	
9/17/1838	John Page	150,000	Bank of U.S. of PA, Athens	150,000	
9/27/1838	John Page	100,000	Bank of U.S. of PA, Athens	100,000	
9/27/1838	R.D.C. Collins	50,000	Bank of U.S. of PA, New Orleans	50,000	
10/10/1838	John Page	125,000	Bank of US of PA, Athens	49,990	
			Bank of US of PA, Nashville	75,010	
			Bank of US of PA, Nashville	73,000	
			Bank of US of PA, Cincinnati	52,000	
10/18/1838	J.P. Simonton	50,000	Collector of New York	50,000	
10/27/1838	John Page	100,000	Collector of New York	100,000	
11/10/1838	R.D.C. Collins	20,000	Bank US of PA, Little Rock	20,000	
11/10/1838	Richard Smith	36,000	Collector of New York	36,000	
11/13/1838	John Page	100,000	Commercial Bank, Cincinnati	10,000	Outstanding
			Savings Institution, Louisville	5,000	Outstanding
			Bank U.S. of PA, New Orleans	30,000	$20K, Outstd.
			Collector of New York	45,000	
11/19/1838	R.J. Meigs	14,489.09	Receiver, Pontotoc, MS	10,000	Outstanding
			Collector of New York	14,489	
11/29/1838	R.D.C. Collins	18,000	Receiver, Little Rock, AR	18,000	Outstanding
11/30/1838	William B. Lewis	11,500	Collector of Philadelphia	11,500	
12/12/1838	R.D.C. Collins	80,000	Bank US of PA, Little Rock	80,000	
12/12/1838	R.D.C. Collins	50,000	Insurance Bank, Columbus, GA	25,000	Outstanding
			Bank U.S. of PA, New Orleans	25,000	Outstanding

List of valuations for Cherokee Improvements, under the treaty of December 29, 1835.

NAMES	VALUATIONS
Kuncheescuneesjer	$ 123.00
Nose cutter	165.00
Oolscuntee	640.00
Dick Nafir	30.00
Quatzy	234.00
Sala Kooka	179.00
Sore Eyed Nancy	111.50
Quatee Bear Head	69.00
Deaf Nancy	108.00
William Griffin	255.50
Eyaw or Pumpkin	70.00
Moses Harris	92.00
Lewis Griffin	1,143.00
Segawee	76.00
John Baldridge	43.50
Tooka	53.00
Tooker	25.00
Kalarksa	1,865.00
John Griffin	1,000.00
Kunchawlee	181.00
Two Fathom	390.50
Oosalilla	18.00
Edward Gunter	21,894.24
Tetawlee	36.00
Allkeenah	58.00
Richard Blackburn	2,110.00
Sally Kehena	36.00
Watt Smith	25.00
Uyawgee	470.00
Polly Smith	115.00
Squotoguska	71.00
Matt M. Seimpsher	2,832.00
Toonosava	422.00
Tegateesha	138.00
William Turner	375.75
Jim Stone	65.00
Hugh Henry	7,042.00
Chusktah	95.00
John R. Nicholson	1,012.00

Jimmy Dry Skul	$ 464.00
David Carter	202.00
Walter Yawhee	117.00
Daniel D. Spencer	2,691.00
Catharine Dorhorty	88.00
James Spencer	1,371.00
Ooalosku	58.00
Robert Lovet	1,332.50
Toosawaltah	145.00
Captain Baldridge	1.296.00
Hairy Jaw	106.00
Old Mrs. Mink	211.00
Heirs of Jack Dorhorty	23.00
Squluhtakee	15.00
Jinny Dorhorty	72.00
Susannah	168.50
George Whitfield	15.00
Chenrske	95.00
Robert Boggs	440.00
Tarapin, or Ticksonka	264.00
Nelly Buffaloe	137.00
John A. Bell	4,630.00
George Sanders	1,057.87 ½
Qualauka	472.50
Nelson or Negrolake	55.00
Hungry Man	36.00
Nelly Kade	40.00
CooSeoo	599.00
Teleeneenahah	441.50
Samuel Gunter	4,833.00
John Otterlifter	308.00
Charles Melton	1,268.00
Watt Sanders	1,903.00
George W. Gunder	2,167.00
Kanantooka	248.00
Rachael Manning	175.00
Widow Saddlebag	130.00
English John	70.00
Sutria	242.00
Stinking Fish	72.00
Oocoosa	191.00
Monkey	80.00
Heuntilaguska	130.00

Bill	$ 64.00
Cheanwee	60.00
Charley	45.00
Arch	58.00
Little Qualauka	25.00
Jesse Levett	81.00
Dollar	85.50
Auley Swimmey	541.12 ½
War Hatcher	170.50
Old Mr. Jeffrey	171.00
Suttur, or Jno. shatur	220.00
Soldier	411.00
Ootalla	84.00
Widow Swee Nees	200.00
Dr. William A. Davis	3,887.00
Teekatock	277.00
James B. Vant	1,220.00
Oosulta	217.00
Thomas Watts	928.00
George	173.50
Robin	608.00
Tarkea	30.00
John Beemer	407.00
Toonowwee	30.00
Peter Parber	60.00
Betsy Halk	224.00
Stephen Jeffrey	246.00
Quooloskee	60.00
Elizabeth Thompson	297.00
George Arnold	146.00
Larkin Bevint	970.00
Oouakahata	85.00
Dry Forehead	531.00
Tooka	104.00
Richard Fields	2,611.00
Fly, or Tecannaulula	340.50
William Lovell	50.00
Heirs of Blackman or Qualka	299.00
Charles Thompson	257.00
Souranooka	110.50
Willaim Parrott	710.00
Jenny Pat	20.00
Caleb Hunt	

Tin Cup	$ 209.00
Nedkinarsheeshee	180.00
Tesuteesku	65.00
Tunie	884.00
Ahauma	73.00
Dick or Tootertetah	239.00
Fire Killer	151.00
Gundagee	246.00
Nanasuee	389.50
Parch Corn	705.00
Oolotoo	93.00
Benj. Merrill	258.00
Coooosta	93.00
Samuel Neal	100.00
Tekugeeska	102.50
Robert Brown	1,569.00
Kaluntanehu	1,089.00
Dausbird Harris	95.00
Chulaskatuhee	110.00
Martin Branham	2,828.25
Kooaloske	59.00
Joseph B. Collins	209.50
Choonstooeh	15.50
Charles Harris	660.00
Eeentie	230.50
George Welch	4,666.75
Toosawaltee	153.50
Sawnee	426.25
Teenaneesku	391.00
Good Money	34.00
Unaketaher	360.00
Star	300.50
George Fallen	497.00
Humming Bird	153.00
Salaauquee	511.00
Akelineka	118.50
Olly	220.50
Sampson	118.50
Bob	114.00
Kunsena	60.00
David Cordery, deceased	1,725.75

Aggy Foster	$ 567.50
John and Sarah Rogers	11,044.50
War Club	617.00
Robert Rogers	2,329.00
Ooltaheka	215.00
Charlotte Vickery	1,997.00
Sarcy	60.00
George W. Walters	7,346.50
Skonatehi	224.50
James Cleland	1,514.00
John Vann	198.00
John Satterfield	1,779.25
Ootelah	291.00
Coteccave	122.00
Howling Wolf	239.00
Betsy Tobacco Boy	45.00
Keeskunter	103.00
John Cahoosu, widow	52.00
Sutta	110.00
Saquawalta	142.00
Anennetto	80.00
Ookanegee	40.00
Cornfield John	225.00
Oucheesah	238.00
Spring Frog	89.00
Johnny Snake	57.50
Tom Murphy	213.00
Johnson Sutta	83.00
Heirs of Kekana Murphy	398.00
Canesauayah	35.00
Chenoquah	212.00
Chauhah, and Tesoneeska	101.00
Standing Turkey	329.00
Sally Snail	36.00
Wagoolah	304.50
Walleah	70.00
Narcissa Munroe	718.175
Turn Over	254.00
Betsy Dougherty	----------
Jack Woodward	490.00
Sallagatahee	103.50
Thomas Foster	164.00
Yonaguskee	47.50

Drowning Bear	$ 1,099.00
Two Dollar	187.25
Arch Wilson	271.50
Sutt	131.00
Sweet Water	692.50
Tahlunteeska	118.75
Chenoika	317.00
Suiecouhei	86.00
Nanny	144.00
Cahoogishei	293.25
Tahluntuska	213.50
Ouletaslee	128.00
David Styner	415.50
Eutaeh	69.50
Big Kettle	267.00
Teke, or Ezekiel	108.00
Johnawanie	325.00
Chuiheitla	54.00
Bull Frog	83.75
Caty	25.00
Tenaleeska	96.50
Bug	33.25
Aka	139.00
Bag	31.00
Choka	47.00
Rain Crow	114.00
Ootie	56.00
Young Duck	113.00
Shadow	37.50
Canawsawsky	196.00
Hog Shooter	56.00
Teseeska	45.50.
Young Bird	347.50
Chua Welk	25.00
John Tater Hair	42.00
Natowee	77.00
Taterhair	170.25
Jug	150.50
Sicktowa	44.00
Kalovahuska	178.50
Jim John	24.50
Jim	83.00
Charles	102.75

Dryer	$ 323.00
Canesky	17.00
Little Tarrapin	174.50
Tesawheoh	16.50
Packston	139.00
Ousawee	72.00
Scaffold	617.00
Bozard Flapper	36.00
Jackson Rattlinggourd	707.50
Whiteman Killer	52.00
Red Bird	217.50
Johnson Christy	132.00
Tiger	1,319.00
Skause	30.00
George	238.00
Sikilley's Widow	112.50
Jack Downing	364.50
Tobacco	105.50
Dew	436.00
Haytayteska	25.00
Thomas Gillispie	2,278.50
Charles	78.00
Toosawatte	883.00
Tooka	84.00
Israel	557.50
Tahchusa	101.00
Charles Butler	482.00
Suttuka	33.00
Sawney	110.00
Star	20.00
Sitting Rock	186.50
Walter	78.00
Sitting Turtle	321.00
Chaueska	56.00
Trunk	76.00
Will Scott	83.50
Deer Head	41.00
Mrs. Stone	124.00
Chune	118.00
Sall	131.00
Warty	167.00
Bill Sour John	153.25
Sitawaker	175.50

Chyauka	$	82.00
Glory		118.00
Kustia		20.00
John Dick		24.50
Jewker		130.00
Robin Downing		84.00
Ellis S. Harlin		4,185.00
Ahlula		92.00
Gardner		359.50
Flat Head		63.00
Rat		182.00
Toonoweh		271.00
Wati Foster		44.00
Jesse Scott		84.00
Will Arnold		554.00
Sucher		96.00
Glory's Heirs		71.50
Chick Sutty		120.00
Cross Cat		261.50
Eli Palmer		211.00
Cylas Palmer		2,786.00
Anna		276.00
Dorcas Dunkin		135.00
Fog		263.00
Waker		41.00
Atawah		261.00
Sam Grasshopper		30.00
Cheeusta		25.00
Watea		30.00
Hawee		61.00
Hyawqua		78.00
Salinqua		158.00
Little Bear		92.00
George English		377.50
Susannah		25.00
Bear's Paw		255.00
Drawing Knife		161.00
Dick Sander's Wife		514.25
Steeler		48.75
Mean Dog		453.00
Sally		47.00
Sitawakee		387.00
Buzzard		104.00

Jack	$ 73.00
John O. Waive	45.00
Davis	47.00
Waster	72.00
Red Bird	33.00
George	169.00
John Chickanaler	142.00
Tooni Sanders	156.00
John Dick	71.00
Thomas Sanders	174.50
Anianka	35.00
Robert Sanders	50.00
Dedaper	234.00
Girl Catcher	194.00
Cloida	85.00
Boiled Corn	75.00
Cotaguskee	128.00
Samuel W. Bell	1,168.25
Thulkulasker	522.75
Bark Taylor	610.75
David Watie	3,754.00
Jack Taylor	198.00
Archil Downing	663.50
William Connor	1,199.00
Ave Vann	90.75
John Ratliff	3,745.40
Gahtuskee	216.00
Betsey Cade	205.10
Artilla Sanders	263.25
Toogertanger, or Stand	65.50
George Ross	175.50
Major Ridge	24,127.00
Calvin Wolf, or Downing	584.50
Samuel Scott	307.00
Kaantusulla	109.00
Charles Moore	2,806.50
Hammer	576.50
David Timpson	326.00
Rattlesnake Moore	311.60
Jim Crabgrass, or White Path	138.50
Reader Moore	361.75
Crying Snake	796.87 ½
Nancy, Crying Snake's Mother	796.87 ½

Elijah Moore	$	295.90
James Starr		1,815.00
Yonah Killer		1,660.00
Widow Watts		432.00
John Fields		832.80
Big Milk		207.50
Archilla Smith		2,275.90
Aggo Smith		303.05
Robert McFier		75.00
Samuel Craig		2,064.50
Nancy Harris		642.75
Tobacco Plant		223.00
Daniel Mills		378.80
Nitts, (son of Sticker)		227.50
Ground Mole		1,909.20
Dick Scott		1,056.40
Estaconna		928.65
Tshunaika		151.00
Brush in the Water		231.25
Spirit, (son of Buffalo Fish)		346.50
John Raincrow		247.00
Tustaree, (son of Sticker)		104.00
Sarah Raincrow		353.00
Tailnka, or Raincrow		667.90
Buffalo Fish		934.25
James McTier		45.10
Testaonee		268.25
Sour Mush		328.80
Sawney Vann		243.50
To-morrow		384.50
Makee, or Peggy		65.00
Kager		546.50
John Martin		16,796.00
B.F. Thompson		9,625.50
Water Guttee		75.00
Joseph M. Lynch		10,806.75
Alsey Swimmer		108.00
James A. Thompson		5,545.00
Eyahtahyah		129.00
George W. Adair		5,098.75
John Longfrost		421.00
Samuel Mays		12,919.00

Eagle Sitting in a Tree	$ 193.00
Daniel McCoy	3,231.00
Alexander Tutt	84.00
Chuqualalaqu	488.00
Joseph Rogers	1,497.00
Peggy, (Widow of Tieskee)	546.75
Lovely Rogers	560.00
Chulcoluskee	1,047.50
Thos. Goss's Orphans	1,846.50
Old Corn Silk	71.00
Joseph A. Foreman	523.00
Tannalshelah Staker	92.25
Lowry Williams	3,073.75
Astahuah	55.00
John Williams	5,098.50
Chicken Cock	184.00
Martin Davis	1,833.75
John	305.00
Susan Jane Harlin	176.00
Assulita	334.25
Johnson Thompson	4,220.50
Teeartoouskee's Orphans	140.00
Thomas B. Adair's Estate	2,867.50
Cartoo, or Bread	399.00
Andrew Adair	3,683.50
William H. Foreman	364.00
Amertoyehah	249.00
Stephen Ray	405.00
Snake, Buffalo Fish's Son	177.25
Peggy Rowe	220.00
Ostahlanah	271.25
Black Bird	240.50
Houghcherkeeskee	35.00
John Fields, Jr.	1,811.00
Long Shell Turtle	446.00
Nancy Bete's Mother	83.25
Oosherlohhee	132.00
Archa Rowe	1,906.50
Jenny Rowe	435.00
Sandy Woodard	258.25
Big Coon, or Standing Wolf	1,126.00
Harry Vann	118.50
Bear Meat, Senior	1,895.00

George Bear Meat	$	762.25
Polly Jack		456.50
John W. West		1,987.00
Thomas Woodward		1,312.00
Johnson Rogers		5,720.00
Ben TeesKee		443.00
Samuel McAman		2,054.50
Guts		324.00
George Fields		1,237.00
Bill Corn Silk		48.75
Ryder Fields		1,441.00
Taeskee		259.30 1/4
Alexander Gilbreath		3,864.00
Ahwattee		144.94 3/4
Thomas F. Taylor		2,295.20
John Brewer		1,860.55
Thomas Brewer		248.80
Daniel J. Ketchum		604.50
Tunnooa		854.00
Fog Ancha Boneater		--------------
Cork Silk, Jr.		287.50
Tom		66.75
John Watermellon		284.75
Samuel L. Bullard		1,489.00
Ear Bob		433.50
Richard Taylor, Jr.		70.00
Toolough		668.50
Oslasoolee		25.00
Alexander Drumgool		1,656.00
Mills		111.00
Joshua Kirkpatrick		938.00
Rising Fawn, or Fawn Killer		90.00
Edward Adair		2,292.00
Ogeeche		344.00
Benjamin F. Adair		663.00
Cabin Smitt's Widow		147.50
Walter V. Adair's Estate		7,732.00
Solonakee		46.00
Samuel Adair		2,031.00
Ned Fawn, or Lee		711.50
Crawler Wicked		684.00
Alexander McKay		12,966.50
Jim Fire Killer		84.75

Jacob Nicholson	$ 2,287.50
John Hilderbrand, Senior	1,333.02 ½
Joshua Buffington	3,667.25
Weelukeekee	857.75
Stephen Graves	1,757.50
Corn Tassell	475.00
Catharine Gann	1,385.50
Toonahgee	108.50
Avery Miller	2,169.50
George Hicks	3,316.50
Koniskooa	231.75
Young Turkey	447.00
Jeremiah C. Towers	2,579.50
Chewgahnalilanah	478.75
David Sanders	1,581.00
Wahyou Killer	161.00
Calvin S. Adair	1,521.00
Tomloweyowka	20.00
James J. Trott	3,357.50
Bread	57.75
Jack Hawkins	1,132.83 3/4
Ulstowestee	116.25
Elias Boudinot	3,917.00
Chewlaskah, or Potts	535.00
Jesse Half-Blood	1,633.50
Leach	160.00
Cheegachawna	139.00
Fishing Hawk	238.50
Jacob West	3,116.00
Red Bird	234.50
Duck Ahtowee	499.00
Little Turtle	946.75
Teesatisha	2,301.50
Dirt Litter	376.60
Robert Sanders	1,947.50
Seeakee	173.25
Collins McDonald	3,306.50
Saweyahlase	225.50
Qeorge Milier	921.50
Moses Lee	242.50
James Cook	200.00
Watt Lee	378.00
Killer Neka	427.50

Josiah	$	160.75
Killer Moore		1,267.50
Richard Guess		300.75
Ala		90.00
Nelly		185.80
Ootahlewtahguah		266.50
Grasshopper		25.00
Liver		176.50
Cart, or Bread		522.75
Funi, a woman		147.50
Cheaneekcok		51.75
Nickate, a woman		633.00
John Alexander		64.00
Charley Fish		487.50
Talahhee		328.25
Peggy Overtaker		377.00
Kikatee		527.50
Polly		139.00
Buffalo		49.00
Nelly		164.00
Toogertanger, or Stand		65.50
Utahtageesher		229.00
Nancy Ketchum		271.75
Hoe		446.50
Charles Justice		915.50
Barrow		375.00
John Smith		130.00
Polly Blackbird		231.00
Ooweskooke, (Charley)		388.25
Cahnatana		200.00
Chateeste, or Pheasant		405.25
Alsa		130.00
Cogerohyohleeskee		466.75
Culsti		336.50
John Walker		84.50
Peggy, Teseskee's Wife		756.00
Partridge Nose		891.50
House Berg		778.00
Aggy Cameron		174.00
Ecooa		365.00
Toonie		330.00
Green Wood		968.00
Thomas Cameron		180.75

Anna Grape	$	124.00
Ahwahheelee, or Eagle		288.50
Fooenoee		495.00
Nayahootagee		177.00
Dorcas		220.00
Vincent Gold		150.60
Charlie		712.50
Tom McLemore		279.75
Catageeskee		470.50
Ben Tarpin, or Trott		142.00
Walka		115.00
Atawhee		73.75
Warsat		56.00
Afsnlatee		92.00
Will		431.00
Long Pigeon		128.00
Crow		527.50
Tesenahee Fealin		1,213.50
Caneka		395.00
Clawyacahnah		350.75
Black Fog		423.00
Tugeeeskee, or Homing Lifton		131.00
Nancy		590.50
Teeteneskee		243.25
Tekahsatagee		390.00
Tankee, (widow)		185.75
Chulixir, or Guts		757.50
Salawanyah		469.50
Will		78.00
Smoke Smith		197.00
Moses		230.00
John Brown		7,110.50
Ooti		202.50
Sig Keeln		581.25
Walking Stick		1,358.00
Tallatoe, or Cricket		409.00
Teeseska		200.00
Elizabeth Elliott		326.25
Johnny Largess		182.00
Narcheah		255.75
Tawgawiskotee		515.50
Astowkee		90.00
William Vann		367.50

Tarcheechee	$	247.50
Cat Fish		170.00
George Lee		188.25
Bull		45.00
Nelly		125.00
Utseeetaee		341.00
John		175.00
Sequanee		94.50
Noisy		70.00
Jesse Barraw		597.70
Tuni		250.50
Squirrel		67.00
Catehe		587.50
White Killer		77.25
Bear Stick		1,026.31 1/4
Oonenakerterker		40.00
Thomas Sanga, or Thomas McCoy		237.25
James Hughs		508.75
Sarah Hughs, wife of Robert Brown		445.87
Edmund Dunkin		1,462.00
Ellis Beck		649.00
Samuel C. Bennett		492.00
Benjamin F. Adair		877.00
Foosawalta, or John Acorn		1,041.50
William Harris		799.00
Susan Harris		700.00
Nancy Miller		47.00
Pheasant Junebug		306.00
Eleck		80.50
Lucy Taylor		200.00
Olehunloice		81.50
Tesateska, or Dew		17.00
Wyaluka		1,114.98
Farnucky, or Horse Fly		480.00
Betsey Thompson		876.00
Tarlossex, or Pass By		415.60
Wiley Karlas-cher		85.50
Cloaka		189.00
Wauchusa		83.50
John Chambers		193.00
Etanteeska		179.00
Asute Ountie, or Lying Fish		33.52

Sally Timberlake	$	97.50
Maxwell Chambers		1,112.45
Kalarchee		713.00
Jesse Mayfield		8,623.50
Chewee		305.00
Alexander A. Clingan		2,022.50
Mrs. Tawney		88.00
Peterson Thomas		337.50
Sarcy		174.50
Tesoogoslia, or Scraper		57.00
Cloontester, or Pheasant		300.00
Lovorina, or Robin		653.00
John an Chuca		470.50
Josinh M. Reece		308.50
Teolsena		29.50
Taleleque, or Grass Hopper		342.50
Blue Bird		20.00
Tshnweeska		214.50
John Fallin		109.60
John Butler		513.00
Ailsy Otterlifter		288.50
Judaqua Neloya, or Fishing Hawk		683.00
Kuikolosskee		283.00
Cronoonoo, or Bull Frog		805.30
Ywayawga		230.75
Andrew Taylor		2,520.50
Lydia Perry		130.50
Jesse Bushyhead		176.00
Suaka		139.50
George Candy		1,612.12 ½
Old Bushyhead		668.00
Sally Buffaloe Head		314.50
Joseph Faller		400.00
Wheynukee		145.50
Jesse Bushyhead		1,614.00
Heirs of John Walker, Jr., deceased		11,555.00
Rev. Isaac Walker		434.25
David M. Harlan		2,241.00
Fire Killer		139.00
James Bigby		1,110.00
James Baldridge		280.50
Stephen Foreman		1,873.50
Robert Burnes		420.00

Cheesu, or Cabin	$	293.50
Pigeon		166.75
Little Anne		22.50
Thomas Barnes		226.00
Peter Miller		598.00
Samuel Parks		3,394.60
Switsler		581.00
Tetakha		455.00
Hallowing Frog		61.00
James C. Price		2,223.00
Young Glass		681.50
George M. Murrell		2,116.00
Young Beaver		185.50
Capt. John Watts		838.00
Whirld Wind		135.00
Corn Tassell		65.00
Auley		151.00
Sally Long Knife		712.14
Hawk		91.00
Teeseeska		505.50
William McAlexander		487.00
Kansutotee		1,407.00
Chunoolusker, or Thomas		62.00
White Man Killer		169.50
Will		62.00
Path Killer		208.25
Caynga		99.00
Richard Benge		207.00
Squitchee		61.25
Ootalahta		192.50
George, or O O Kestee		67.00
Alnehna		204.00
Widow Thompson		231.00
Elly		223.50
Whirlwind		190.75
Lenmel Childress		3,356.50
Hard		51.00
Salenqua, or Muskrat		614.50
Nancy Benge		100.00
Kalogolaqua, or Big Hoe		227.00
Hunter Lang		96.00
Goose Lang		311.50
Nick Sanders		581.25

Sankennah	$	669.50
O Oskulska		103.00
Noon Day		147.00
Kannontooe		210.25
Archibald Lowray		341.40
Squonto		99.00
Jenny Hog		142.00
O O Kahunta		20.00
Widow McPherson		314.50
Talustoeska		75.00
Heflip		269.00
Flemuel childress		563.00
July		689.00
Big Wolf		102.00
Nanny		121.00
Robin Perry		47.00
Catherine North		171.00
Feather		30.00
Martin North		225.00
Uneekatakee		72.00
Scrape Shins		380.50
James McNair		2,692.25
James Qnalquah		447.00
Johnson Foreman		1,660.50
Barrowtenna		163.00
James Vane		97.81
Weeloogah		538.00
Kuntoleeco, or Clapboard		241.00
Ellick Pike		107.75
Nancy Faught		256.00
Olla, David Miller's Wife		324.00
Partridge		314.50
Edmund Fawling		823.00
Amaly		169.25
Ellis Fallen		167.00
Archa Taka		377.75
Nelly Fallen		169.00
Wataneeta, or Weever		545.50
Wassa, or Long Moose		152.00
Red Bird		400.50
Jesse McLain		1,079.50
Leaf Bon		275.00
Howeeka and Young Deer		419.00

Tetanoskee	$ 169.00
Prusia Fourman	60.00
Talateska	756.00
James Spears	1,187.50
George Bow	287.00
Whanett, or Young Wolf	150.00
Carlooneheskee	125.00
Black Bird	326.50
Stand Bow	235.00
Kunkatoka, or Standing Turkey	392.50
Little Meat	381.00
Koneskusko, or theft	24.00
Sayweenee	337.50
Lame Davy	60.00
Checooah	247.00
Choola John	177.50
Ruth Buffington	355.50
Squahmdah, or Young Pig	40.00
Amartuskah	291.75
Lewis Ross	25,980.75
James Sanders	659.25
Pisse	40.00
Small Back	701.50
John Soon in the Morning	85.00
Swan	371.00
Secunda, or Young Deer's Trip	48.00
Scalp	311.50
Bird	342.00
Smoke	215.00
Alumn	6.00
Twonegha	758.00
Moses	1.00
Nancy Leaf	300.00
David Wilterbrand	811.00
Bonery	198.50
Hiram McCrary	388.75
Widow Fields	38.00
Taluska	169.50
Leaf	16.00
TetaKeeska	115.50
Rouge	388.00
Walter Lizard	325.87
Stool's Heirs	194.00

Mickatocka	$ 346.25
Smoke	606.00
Thompson Downing	440.50
Little Hair	501.75
Johnson	72.00
Big Field	286.10
Lucy	96.50
Widow Murphy	289.50
Nicholas B. Mihair	6,097.00
Toney Ratling Gourd	103.00
James Helterbrand	706.00
Widow Crutchfield	174.50
George Helterbrand	1,035.75
Standing Man	240.25
Tyeeska	42.50
Jesse Cade	33.00
Koonetoo	196.00
Samuel W. Bell	1,805.21
Moses Helterbrand	212.75
John G. Ross	4,517.00
Ned Brams	210.00
Jack Duck	45.00
Arch Spears	256.00
Possum	10.00
Karsawnak	231.00
Hungry	111.75
Susannah	445.50
Archibald Acron	393.00
Bridge Maker	796.00
Walatooga	396.75
Thomas Sahkeyah	70.00
Nancy Spears	192.50
John Bell	3,062.50
Saucy Boy	35.00
James Lamar, or Nicholson's Heirs	695.50
Michael Helterbrand	13,221.00
Hirum Sandrum	20.50
Ootaheeta	79.00
Anderson Springston	191.00
Samuel McMusnon	88.00
James Martin	101.00
Choctaw Killer	246.25
Stephen Helterbrand	294.00

Stinking Fish	$	277.75
John Catron		706.00
Knight Killer		81.00
Dick Wilson		120.50
Big Dollar		263.00
Ahusetas Rah		10.00
John Skul		275.00
ChutaKah		155.00
Egg		10.00
Joseph Cookson		1,001.00
Oelonehsteska		406.75
Tyana Widow Pigeon		116.00
Sally Fisk		179.25
Lewis Tynmer		21.50
Old Trunk		25.50
Elizabeth Downing		349.25
Jumper		416.25
Levina Bean		26.50
Bull Snake		218.25
Pigeon Out of Water		3.00
Light Toter		481.15
Pigeon In the Water		129.50
John F. Boots		857.75
Calenahaaska		78.00
Archa Big Feather		30.00
Bud		146.00
John Orrnah		656.25
SawteeChee, or W. Wilson		408.00
Step About, or Tallaham		381.00
Biter		113.50
Sally Scraper, Wife of Tho. Terman		---------
Thomas Teemer		374.50
Johnson		50.00
Joseph Blackban		429.75
King Fisher		278.50
Diver		69.50
Smoke		583.50
Nancy		85.00
Cheeva		298.50
Jack Smoke		210.00
James Canotitah		56.00
Charles Smoke		146.00
Old Culsowa		122.50

Tread About	$	630.25
Nelson Orr		89.00
David McNair		12,220.25
George Lowry, Jr.		1,021.25
Jack Tawney and others, Heirs of Kansahela		296.50
Big Feather		309.00
Conesawlewah		198.00
Sinew		390.00
Chicoleska		157.00
Widow Wheeler		518.37 ½
Johny T.		10.00
Jack Justice		16.37 ½
John Mackintosh		487.62 ½
Kalota		93.25
James P. Lowry		2,148.15
Kalloway		33.00
Corn Tassel		356.00
Jaloiika		48.00
Charles McIntosh		389.50
Frog		37.00
John Purlone		695.00
Tekorqueona		62.00
Peggy Stephens		130.00
O. Salmon		25.00
Goose Langley		191.50
Toowatalata		61.50
Chee Chee		377.87 ½
Horn		6.00
Jesse Stephens		149.00
Tarlenetomakah		50.00
Martin Benge		406.00
Stooping Deer		137.00
Widow Locust		400.25
Yauyouskah		143.00
Widow Thompson		319.00
Tartulana		111.50
Richard Keys and Heirs of Samuel Keys		990.50
Eyawyouska		24.00
Mrs. Price's Heirs		877.50
Tyeeska		109.75
Mary Doherty		1,665.00
Shadow		54.00
David Gauge		4,289.79

Tesateeska	$ 68.00
Nelson Harlan	1,008.25
George Baldridge	1,849.47 ½
Sally Lamar	4,708.50
Greasy, or Corcha	62.25
John Huss	861.18
Oohstooah	68.00
John McCoy	608.00
Cowwaneta	50.00
Sally	411.55
Water Lizard	40.50
Widow Justice	509.50
Choonstoostee	41.00
Anderson Lowry	1,407.50
Atawa	108.50
Rachael Orr	302.00
William Dennis	99.00
George Lowry, Jr.	2,863.50
Samuel Martin	531.50
John Cowert	1,434.50
Concheesteeche	709.50
Elizabeth Pach	4,957.55
Uwaka	54.00
Salola	122.00
James Orr	750.75
Noocheewee	183.50
Roasting Bear	639.00
Whaka	956.25
Wins Blow, or John Bear	339.00
Smoke	329.00
Moses Camron	15.00
Mink Watts	319.00
Jane Bark	384.50
Sarah Hix, Wife of Wm. Hix	5,138.00
Lee, or Rising Fawn	986.50
Foialeesa	638.00
Moses Lee	47.00
Mika	289.50
David Downing	----------
Jesse Lea	98.00
Drowning Bear	107.00
Charlaerhee	302.50
Screech Owl	198.00

Fish Tail	72.00
Feeeskeeska	301.00
Culstye	735.71 ½
Joseph Spears	284.00
William Grimmett	1,907.77
Uyawseeska	8.00
Runabout Scraper	207.00
Poor Shoat	403.00
Soft Shell Turtle, or doonowee	286.00
Tick String	1,358.50
Jonathan Mulkey	1,344.25
Hiram Linder	916.00
Quatee	97.50
Levi Baily	697.15
Mosey	408.50
Peter Helterbrand	11,211.73
James Chambers	293.50
Two Rods	79.00
George Chambers	4,186.09
Charley Root	232.50
Talla Seena	607.84 ½
Big Mush	330.50
Edward Fry	1,699.25
Onion in the Pot	53.37 ½
Pole Cat	872.25
Standing Turkey	76.50
Dog Wood	513.10
Anuhahee	94.00
Frog	650.00
John Helterbrand	19.97 ½
Richard Ratliff	157.00
Skouse	20.00
Charles H. Vance	1,349.25
Nelly Pain	231.50
Charley Teeler	78.00
Johnee Catawbee	168.50
Anna Augur Hole	93.00
George Starr	3,338.50
George Augur Hole	74.00
Arch Buffalo	175.25
Sanders Choate	109.00
Caty Buffalo	239.00
Beaver Tail	569.00

Soulder	$	40.00
Jenny Path Killer		838.50
Eentie		69.00
George Campbell		1,110.00
Swimmer		250.00
Turner		747.00
Mouse Paine		131.00
Money Hunter		772.86
Sally Persimmon		66.00
Nancy Snake		65.00
Nicy Helterbrand		35.00
Jackson		30.00
John Wilson		56.00
Widow Pumpkihop		2,208.00
Sawney, or Dianah		106.00
Geroge Gunpile's brother		632.00
Kanutza		110.00
Gunpile		75.00
John Tawwue		208.50
Caty, Jim Lasley's wife		428.75
Will,		39.00
James Lasley		8,009.15
Deer Head		310.50
Wonenah		207.60
Jo Deer Head		13.00
Ann Path Killer		408.00
Widow Pheasant		71.50
Tetenusker		204.30
Snake Tail		277.50
Tenewee		191.80
Wasp Catcher		68.50
Tuny		104.00
Crow		43.50
Young Wolf		140.25
Ketcher		304.50
Tassel Nail		77.00
Tyesska		96.50
Bear Ponch		15.00
Sarcy		32.50
Richard Ratliff, Jr.		1,683.50
Spring Mouse		134.00
Takey		401.00
Tuckalawsee		34.00

Lucy Ratliff	$ 520.00
Crazy Man	41.00
Charles Neeleka	217.50
Uluteeska	21.00
LeCowee	43.00
Anny Old Woman	61.00
Ueskeena	25.00
Biter	30.00
Farley	28.00
Rachael Bright	166.50
Cat	5.00
Tar Chanchee	110.00
Whaaka	252.00
Betsy Kenner	177.00
Crawler	153.25
Skeyownieker	107.00
Howling Wolf	146.25
T.A. Rey	107.25
Nantawogo	83.00
Houston	2,148.75
Little Wood	92.00
Ahnonhee	186.50
Teskegatahe	113.00
Jee	119.75
Lowze	72.50
Black Beard	249.00
Culquolosker	107.50
Tuoonteskey	525.50
Oolsartargeesa	3.00
Sequahter	223.00
Heuntologeeska	93.50
Dirt Seller	482.50
Skunti	34.00
Samuel Ratliff	292.00
Tunateeska	306.50
Anna Hyeant	200.00
Wilson	147.50
Buffalo	468.50
Coononoo	40.00
Head Toter	61.00
Kartoo	167.00
Seiter	159.00
Tunantuee	117.00

Black Jack	$ 10.00	
Lucy	25.00	
Cekeookuekee	507.00	
teeseeska, or Sarah	33.00	
Naynee	497.50	
Ooleesawlee	85.50	
Tunneah	75.00	
Carles Quallen	4.00	
Pigeon Fife Killer	89.00	
Arquoneeska	92.00	
Rachael		41.00
Tekaneeska	57.00	
Wipemiass	479.00	
Bird Choper	215.00	
Shade	225.50	
Chowauqua	33.00	
Tarkagee	1,683.00	
Connegoweska	39.00	
Charley	30.00	
Oowaata	50.00	
Grits	859.00	
Chuluah	186.00	
Feather	50.00	
Kikotokee	389.00	
Cekekee	240.00	
Martin	148.50	
Walking Wolf	294.00	
Tooyah	159.50	
Shite Poke	128.50	
Chickoohee	129.00	
Feasant	345.00	
Lubelanagess	43.00	
Eli Smith	348.00	
Sartanah	64.50	
Burnt Rail	35.00	
Kartoquilla	112.50	
Man Killer	212.00	
Kuth Koner	35.00	
Mushroom	267.50	
Cowalateeska	36.00	
Nance	625.00	
Charley Downing	491.00	
Nooata	70.00	

William Blue Calf	$ 302.50
Anahalee	32.50
Cooper	1,263.00
Weela	64.00
Bark Floot	1,111.87 ½
Staff	106.00
Mrs. Brown	18.00
Wolf Track	90.00
Sally Bennet	52.00
Betsey Coker	168.50
White Tobacco	362.00
Seneca	101.50
Fox Fire	325.00
Coker George	165.50
Squirl	20.00
Sally	20.00
Mills	134.00
Kaateekh	208.00
George White Tobacco	153.00
James Kateekah	10.00
Teesertoousky	90.00
Kankaleeska	183.50
Head Thrower	214.00
Johny Wainey	76.00
Chicken	20.00
John Mole Cat	100.00
Six Killer	81.00
Souldier	32.00
Tansle Camel	314.40
Karsalta	20.00
Jackson Man Killer	300.00
J. Hicks	331.00
John Watts	448.00
Cheyawsee	137.00
Scraper	1,907.00
Tyyeker	1,408.00
Moses Harris	68.00
Kuncheestaneeska	123.00
Samuel Downing	546.00
Eleanor Downing	307.00
James Crittendon	652.00
Archey Vann	88.00
Dick Tucco	125.00

David Downing	$ 225.75
Tucco	151.00
Dock Tucco	80.00
Drowning Bear	35.00
Rock	187.00
Chickanailer	15.00
Big Bean	42.50
Jim Downing	225.00
Widow Winn	209.00
Toater	90.00
Coosalowa	181.00
Jesse Cockran	250.00
William Davis	102.75
Snipe, or Colostola	360.00
Sconti	235.00
Big John (deceased)	523.00
Toyaleesa, or Beaver Toater	138.25
Cloud	223.50
Ailsey Cockran	33.00
Young Turkey	23.50
James Dougherty	392.50
Moses Dougherty	100.00
Edward Wicked	149.00
John Proctor, Jr.	335.50
John Proctor, Sr.	480.00
Child Toater	139.50
Skynke	203.50
Squanny Cole	64.00
Charles Vickory	100.00
Elizabeth Welch	442.00
William Bean	215.75
Buzzard Flapper	428.50
Charles Snipe	81.00
Old Snipe	393.00
George Still	2,160.50
Jack Still	2,248.75
Dorcas' (Kaskaloska's Wife)	45.00
George Tenna	93.00
David Downing	224.25
Tarlontiska	79.00
Pan	66.00
Child Toater (Esowa)	165.50
White Killer	201.50

Tuckanesene, or his wife, Dorcas	143.50
Ailsey's children, Tawney and Ailer	72.00
Old Lecher	98.00
Sally Blackwood, (Jeo's Wife)	64.00
Little Soap	130.00
Up the Branch	154.00
Old Chewa	702.50
Blowja	139.00
Templeton, or Taewaryer	103.00
Jesse Brewer	174.00
Tekoniska	613.50
Good Dollar	32.00
Arquaria	29.50
Sally, (Nancy Woddall's Mother)	101.00
Old Oosemda	90.00
Elizabeth and Hetty Pott	25.00
Dickeski	559.00
Hickkitowa	47.75
Peach Eater	279.25
Jinney	87.00
Archi Killa	251.50
Sartake	163.75
Fishing Hawk	32.00
Chick Killa	20.00
Setting Down Bear	193.00
Rotten Man	227.00
Ruth Beck	561.00
Old Tenna	340.00
New Gin and Ben Vann	320.00
Sally Swimmer	55.25
Nelson Tenna	164.00
Crazy Will	23.00
Oolaner, or Lost Man	138.00
Coon	187.25
Swimmer	287.00
Tieski	567.00
Double Tooth, or Teachary	418.75
Ooti	31.00
Aggy, or Agley Sleeve	474.00
John Leecher, Jr.	60.00
Netowa	107.50
Nelly	50.00
Tassell, or Tassell Stoop	137.00

Susanah	$ 277.50
Siccowa	293.00
John Wayne	151.00
Johnny Wayne, Jr.	28.00
Robin Sleaves	446.50
Sally Bee Hunter	634.75
John R. Daniel	1,208.50
Bull, or Cow	231.00
Nancy, Catharine, Jane, thomas, and Walter Daniel	1,105.50
Dun Bean	94.00
Young Turkey	55.00
Old Sharp	130.00
Charles	90.50
Ridge	224.00
Johnny Wayne	287.00
Charles Hammond	364.50
Flying Smith	103.00
Line Fish	341.00
Tetawla	15.00
Weaver	19.00
Jesse Sanders	165.75
Sparrow Hawk	350.50
Dujesta	212.50
James Tenna	156.00
Old Soap	428.00
Corholuga	77.00
Tom Tit	489.50
George Peach Eater	61.25
Robert Berry, deceased	573.62 ½
Spring Frog	360.50
Elizabeth Ragsdale	149.50
Echawcha	82.00
James Timson	126.75
Jimmy Harnidge	775.50
Tom Killer	369.50
Thomas Tom Killer	41.87 ½
Kishikon	180.50
Adam, or Artowa	408.00
Benjamin Ragsdale	122.50
Eleanor Ragsdale	1,157.85
Widow Martin	177.00
Dickeski	231.00
Sally Harnidge	190.75

Ignatius A. Few	$	128.50
Kacyoha		48.00
Jesse		45.50
Blossom		96.50
Bill Still		71.00
Ned Still		648.25
Suaata		137.25
Jug		227.00
Ephraim Rustybelly		194.00
Arley		20.00
Dinah		62.00
Sunday and Polly, (his wife)		74.00
Jim Green and Cook		144.50
Moses Daniel		1,343.37 ½
Tadpole		405.50
Sampson		148.00
Moses Downing		1,127.00
Aaron Downing		535.40
Koosescooe		461.75
Bear Paw		166.50
Rusty Belly		331.00
Polly		70.00
Smoke		247.75
Hog Head		228.75
Jesse Downing		163.50
Old Bear		355.00
Little Tom Killer		457.50
Stinger		316.50
Charley		62.50
Jack		192.50
Chicken		100.00
Arch		111.00
Dreadful Water		249.00
Tarrapin Sitting Down		101.00
Harry Stinger		250.00
Old Sitting Down		148.00
Chewakika		175.50
Old Rising Town		115.50
Wat Sitting Down		69.00
Swinnacauta, (Sitting Down's Old Wife)		187.00
Swimmer		45.00
Techaweeka, or Waster		41.00
Awnerly		25.00

Kilby, or Witch	$ 105.00
Stop	429.00
Poor Bear	340.50
Chowawha	111.00
Good Woman, (a man)	36.00
John Lugeesky	123.00
Oochala	136.00
Waity	251.50
Tompson	279.00
Kulinaka, or Big Acorn	72.00
Illinoika	547.50
Old Sugeeska	70.00
Otter Lifter	101.00
Big Rising Fawn, or Rising Fawn	218.50
Tetenauska	55.00
Watta	137.00
Davy	316.00
George Kala, or Proctor	485.00
Crow	31.50
Turkey and Tail	70.50
Dear Head	34.00
James Proctor	234.25
Nelowa	326.50
Nicholas Proctor	155.00
Sugar John	40.00
Chicken Snake	72.00
Sisty	124.85
Key and Mother	149.00
Pigeon	84.50
Charley and Mother	25.50
Jack Laughing Girl	182.00
Skewanna, or Six Killer	232.00
Cloud	102.00
White Killer	170.00
The Laughing Girl	567.00
George and Mother	15.00
Tarrapin Head	108.00
Sticcahawta	137.00
Sticccahuska	68.00
James Saunders	207.50
Ezekial Ragsdale	166.00
Old Blanket	209.00
Thomas Blanket	20.00

Tenna	$	297.00
Owl and Mother		351.25
Nonnatla		37.00
Anne Wakey		---------
Old Rising Fawn		74.00
Standing Fence		114.00
Wolf's Wife and Children		80.00
John Still		181.50
Sannacowa		93.50
Wood Lark		274.00
Sarah and Coate		62.00
Tahkenawheelee		116.50
Corn Eater		179.00
Coaneta		38.75
Chewee		38.75
Sarah, widow of Chewee		38.75
Leaf		38.75
Anney		38.75
Wakey		38.75
Tooney		38.75
Peggy		38.75
Ann Wakey		38.75
Big Dave		133.00
Senalla		346.00
Sleepy Man		284.00
Young Chicken		379.00
Jack Winn		176.00
Dave Conna		73.00
Ellis		32.00
Johnson, Sally, Aggy, and Moses Alberty		608.50
Knockerman, (John)		80.00
Dorcas Still		35.00
Six Killer		130.00
Cahucca, (Dick, Pritchetts, Mo.)		221.00
Sitting Down Bear		20.00
John Pritchett		147.00
Negro Leg		77.00
Tarcheechee		6.00
Adam		182.00
Jim Groves		70.00
Choachuka		204.50
Willis Hendricks		243.00
Tyena		113.50

Saucy Jack	$ 69.00
Tom Killer	86.00
Toosawalter and Mother	187.00
Washington's Wife	43.00
Falling	68.00
Andrew Saunders	1,295.00
Harry Crittenden	617.00
David Saunders	305.00
George Saunder's Heirs	1,269.50
John Saunders	2,374.50
Samuel Saunders	497.00
Overtaken	103.00
John Dobb	31.00
Joshua	63.00
Tom Pritchett	270.00
William Pritchett	339.50
Wauscutta	302.75
Suwaka Pritchett	152.00
Burnt Wood	116.00
Hugh Montgomery	133.00
Young Duck	136.00
Oolscuntney	180.50
Taarsta, or Catayostah	153.50
Alexander Downing	441.50
Bill Vann	93.00
James Hendricks	210.00
Tobacco Pouch	131.50
Wagon	29.50
Small Back	88.00
Eave Dropper	199.00
Jackson	170.00
The Blackbird	228.00
Mole	20.00
Shot Anow (known as Peter)	265.00
Buck	152.00
Fox Skin	327.00
Jack Downing	143.00
Konorteski	212.75
King Fisher	101.00
Daniel Grasshopper	120.00
Big Coat	128.00
Kullalutta	251.00
Keehuaga, or Dick	96.00

Augoonaneechee, (a woman)	$ 206.00
Anna	60.00
Sarah	192.25
Jim King Fisher	263.50
George	51.00
Ailsey	104.00
John King Fisher	195.00
Cold Weather	444.00
John King Fisher's young wife	119.00
Will	32.00
Allgone	114.00
Cheesetand, or Crawfish	187.00
Johnson	56.00
Tzcowechake	50.50
Chaluski, or Pot	97.50
Bird	166.00
Tackling, or Tesawhiskey	114.00
Sam	50.00
Ookatona, or Big Smoke	75.00
Jailer	39.00
Carley Tehe	98.00
Doublehead	124.00
Chopper, or Cullyer	162.00
Worm	92.00
John Tate	8.00
Charles Downing	191.00
James Proctor	171.50
Frost	26.00
Sockira, or Susan	70.00
Poor Man, or Olasaught	116.00
Turkey	176.00
Peggy Smith, (deceased)	218.00
Betsey Smith	162.75
Richard Crittendon	65.00
Chichsaahee	365.00
Betsey Wolf	339.00
Charley Tehee	535.25
Arlee	174.50
Jane Love	133.00
Nat	40.00
Qualaucha	50.00
Chewaluka	97.50
Caty Eagle	69.00

Kenakwheele	$	179.50
Nancy Stealer		457.00
Ooloocha		321.75
Charles Dobbins		237.50
Sequeechy		337.50
Eli Wolf		50.00
All Bones		284.00
Chenuckeva		40.00
Waky		16.00
Sampson		356.50
Blinkey		352.00
Oolscuntney, or Fool		372.00
Nick Grasshopper		110.00
Kenoskeesha, or Stealer		289.50
James Downing		270.00
William Downing		284.00
William Proctor		717.50
Sitawakee		134.50
Pedro Garcia, or Spanish Peter		246.50
Nancy Still		1,087.00
Sally Still		133.50
George Still		6,305.00
Joseph Proctor		236.75
Tom Winn		110.50
Seed or Blanket		77.75
Girl Killer		100.25
Tom		299.50
Sam		45.50
Skitata		30.00
Charle Tehee		42.75
Tawney, (a woman)		30.00
Dorser, or Mosquito		109.50
Tobacco Hoe		40.00
Walking Stick		179.00
Samuel Tehee		517.00
Nawcheeah		212.00
Staulontus		102.00
Tedahquanner		138.50
Young Chicken, or Chicken Crown		219.75
Chewnonner		185.50
Tail		433.00
Pogoleeska, or Ground Eater		104.00
Goluchee		85.00

Riddle	$ 265.00
Connehana, or Big Head	81.00
Crier	260.00
Old Tobacco	207.50
Betsey King	44.00
Akey Ground Hog	104.75
Naked Man	324.00
Yalhasalah	109.00
Bear Toater	120.25
Conososka	299.75
Young Duck	200.50
Secowey	60.00
Little John	272.00
Skyuka	174.50
Wolf Tacker	32.00
Sitting Bear	60.00
Chicksatahee	15.00
Susannah and Alsey	280.00
Hemp	306.75
Rattler	57.00
Foster Tacanty	122.00
Old White Path	134.50
Rattler, 2d	66.75
Conlakee	80.50
Heirs of Harry Downing and Wife	296.00
Sunday, or Quadahquaskee	110.00
Lace Christy	155.00
George Christy	264.00
Hatchet	232.50
Twist	181.00
Tene Tete	126.00
Old Bushyhead	222.00
Young Bushyhead	190.00
Coluwee	55.00
Cat Fish	255.50
Outlenjowwee, (Skyuke's son)	103.00
Big Bear	126.00
Widow Coats	56.00
Grites	158.50
Eower, Young Wolf's Son	93.00
Nany and Ailsey Bushyhead	262.00
Widow Bear Paw	221.00
Saw Coats	158.00

Big Bear's Mother	$ 161.00
Cock Roaster	78.00
Young Chickalala	78.50
Beaver Toater, or Tayaleese	140.50
Beaver Toater's Wife	106.00
Sceauger	329.00
Old Wolf	157.50
Tauney (a woman)	156.00
Galoskaloya	95.00
Oakshenantee, or Deaf Man	138.00
Little Bird	242.00
Brand	205.00
Sukey	102.00
Jinney	178.00
Mockasin	44.75
Old Tough	76.00
Beaver Toater	30.00
Water	121.50
Rattle Gourd	277.50
Wash Face	102.25
Scongatee	90.50
Tom	133.50
Suchlowga	212.00
Wilson Suwaga and Wife	196.00
Dick Elk	100.50
Big Elk	168.00
Talekee	40.00
Notowakee	147.00
Robin, or Sowany	66.00
Ned and Anley	190.00
Spiller	234.00
Nancy	117.00
Hog, or Lequah	85.00
Dave	85.00
Sautalawock	92.00
John Ross	17,965.75
John Beamer	800.81 1/4
Arch Simmons	309.00
Seguimey Smith	490.00
Sonna Cooyah	163.00
One Eyed Jenney	----------
Olleka and caty	538.50
Billy Hawk	488.00

Henry Nave	$ 6,157.00
Dirty Belly and turkey Lifter	104.50
John Hogg	813.50
Lydia, widow of Deer in the Water	237.25
John Elliott	1,420.00
Lewis Ralston	3,406.00
Thomas Carey	1,557.00
Benjamin F. Adair	877.00
Josiah Hawk	112.25
James Brown	300.00
James Calogee	20.75
William McTear	237.00
Sutleggy	183.00
Turtle Fields	1,690.00
Cheenahwee	525.00
Cat Fields	290.00
Cootiah	46.50
Hawk Baldridge	346.25
Dirt Thrower	484.50
Young Puppy	950.00
Nelly	58.50
Isaac Nicholson	10.00
Tohteecahnahkag	522.00
Olly Lassley	473.15
Astu Askee	79.00
James Fields	2,520.00
Aaron Wilkinson	842.25
William Dameron	400.00
Busy Head	61.00
John Countryman	553.00
Black Fox	237.25
Hammer's Wife	386.00
Dick Wilkinson	139.50
Wahlameta	2,360.50
Cheenohgee	458.50
Sally Hughes	6,226.00
TeecooyeesKee, or flint	98.75
Little Jim	513.00
Good Money	101.75
Crow, or Cheemugah	230.50
John Goodmoney's Son	131.50
Tenooa	352.50
Clohquohlohtoh	139.00

Estate of Chooa	$ 675.50
Cahskahneehe	175.00
Cunseena	233.00
Betsey Rowe	335.00
Young Bird	150.00
Stand Wattee	2,392.00
Three Killer	295.00
Isabella Wattee	2,095.00
AhleeChah	191.50
Widow Squirrel	518.50
Susannah Flea	281.00
Old	546.00
Jonas Broom	140.75
Pigeon Half-Breed	1,125.00
Long Nancy	311.00
Captain Broom	481.00
The Badger	214.00
Casguattre	108.00
Bear Paw	215.00
Singer	81.50
Tooquahtah, or Crawfish	393.72
Walter S. Adair	8,269.50
Drowning Bear	602.25
Teda	640.00
Eli Scott	238.87 ½
Happy Jack	437.00
Wahseehee	145.25
Chikalela	372.00
Doublehead	20.00
Back Bone	300.50
Wooska	300.00
Bear Head	41.00
Tooni	287.00
Batt	303.00
Stand-up	24.00
Oohmemeitooyee	150.50
Young Soap	301.50
Oohohclawyee	139.00
Charly	539.00
Caytee	125.75
Water Killer	171.00
Toosawalta	237.25
Six Killer	150.00

Widow Darney	$ 100.00
Sawyer	190.00
Spring Frog	625.75
Ahchotahe	1,244.00
John	237.00
Teesasky	160.00
Potts	279.50
Oolootsa	80.00
Toonahyee	262.00
Leaf	201.00
Hernett	86.50
Takanaseena	520.00
Fife Turkey	280.75
Tarchersy	372.00
Seed	647.00
Seentahee	588.00
David Canseeme	425.00
Wood Cock	331.25
Teechataesska	370.00
Jack Grimmitt	370.35
Pipe	97.50
UcSaquah	210.25
Nahlahustee	50.00
Suday Cooyah	26.75
Telassheeska	372.00
Water Diver	346.50
Teemalaeesta	41.00
Soft Shell Turtle	185.00
Temaska	41.50
Wolf	1,706.00
Chemaquah Wolf	55.00
Steve Cheelie	75.00
Young Dog	39.00
John Walking Stick	216.00
Lewis Blackburn	9,263.00
Ola Fire	75.00
James Kell	1,521.50
Alfred H. Hudson	4,913.50
Old Nancy	372.25
Samuel Taylor	25.00
Nathan Wolf	50.00
Seteyeah	325.00
Ashes	228.00

Cahtahquilta	$ 170.00
Cheekelteehee	116.00
Tiene Pumpkin	182.00
Teeeeskee	237.50
Cahnawsaska	135.00
Nancy	21.50
Chicken Snake	133.00
Brush	44.50
Washington Lowry	455.00
John D. Wanie	261.50
Nancy	130.05
Jack Miller	1,131.75
Ketcher	286.00
Richard Bogg	1,131.75
White Path	286.00
Waskee	20.00
Ned Crittenden	246.50
Peter Miller	20.00
Poor Boy	246.50
John A. Goddard	115.50
Tumbler	30.00
Nancy Justice	198.00
Betsey	75.00
William Holmes	182.00
Alcy	217.50
Thomas Fox Baldridge	100.00
Judge Henry	310.00
John Young	569.00
Chucheechee	811.00
Smoke Glass	47.00
Ahmee	249.00
Charles Staffle	136.30
Fox	38.00
George Dryhead	50.00
Jo Beanstick	360.00
Richard Brown	297.55
Catowee	161.00
James McPhearson	85.00
Charle Tehee	919.00
Big Jack	326.00
Chooie	514.00
Sally Loury	103.34 1/4
Ookasata	331.00

Archy	$	444.00
Aka		16.00
Wyhooska		2,249.33 1/3
Chesnut		25.00
Widow Wildcat		196.50
Ground Squirrel		75.00
Eskawat		699.00
Black George		43.00
Arseekeeta		574.50
Peggy Moore		410.00
Heirs of Westley Jones		470.00
Jack McPhearson		1,321.00
Tom Pottit		420.00
George Waters		56.00
Jack Fish		305.00
Rattle Gourd Waters		27.00
Chickea, a woman		413.00
Water Lizzard		421.50
Santa Take		144.00
Ned Fire Killer		77.00
Ooloochy		210.00
Pheasant		296.58
Lightning Bug		75.00
Spring Frog		15.00
Ola Bird		70.00
Dreadful Water		85.00
Hommany		280.00
Simblin		30.00
Congolawhattie		181.50
Isaac Walker		551.25
Ostaneunta		250.00
Poerhowwee		106.90
Back Bone		295.00
Red Bird		89.50
Toosawallata		254.50
Deed		333.00
Little Bird		167.50
High Walker		618.00
Choomacheca		60.00
Teetawaw		73.00
Cross Eyed Watt		180.00
Stephen Haynes		20.00
Chowewka's estate		224.00

Nancy Timberlake	$	609.00
Teene		318.50
Widow Big Bear		369.50
Cunseema		189.00
Sweet Water		20.00
Ahtooeska		50.00
Thomas Starr		527.00
Oochasa		139.00
Kaeetza		118.00
Teekaeeska		376.00
Alexander Nave		1,880.25
Dick		712.00
Bain Frog		153.75
Annawaka		194.50
Richard Timberlake		2,094.00
Cahchaseaneesca		81.00
Sarcy		158.50
Taleeska		445.00
Young Pheasant		10.00
Choo chuc		100.00
Kawcha		218.00
Oote		250.51
Cow		150.00
Nancy		181.50
Widow Dirt Seller		161.00
Teedama		322.50
Drowning Bear		80.00
Wahyeokilla		73.00
Manstriker		237.00
Charletehee		177.50
Eliza Maw		1,721.67
Edward Graves		6,652.75
William Rogers		1,391.00
Johnson Fields		239.00
Ah Nelly		758.50
Chererconseelee		132.50
Charles Griffin		1,271.50
William Downing		72.00
Joseph Starr		532.00
Ellis Hogner		32.00
Dennis Wolf		768.00
Widow Graves		408.50

Daniel Griffin	$ 1,495.05
John Doherty	284.00
Soup Smith	20.00
Widow Hogner	192.50
Wallis Vann	591.50
Leaf Doherty	160.00
Walter McDaniel	252.75
Cartso, or Bread	100.00
Stop	560.00
Nan	84.75
Cuntaka	194.50
Wash Burns	44.00
Tom McDaniel	636.00
Ash Hopper	479.00
Bill McDaniel	60.00
Blue Lizzard	92.00
Fox Taylor	894.50
Auqua	79.75
Six Killer	440.00
Wood Cock	258.00
Chualeoka	503.50
Pheasant	396.50
James P. Chislom	185.00
William Beamer	209.00
Johnson Murphy	342.00
John Ridge	19,741.67 ½
Alfred Scudder	2,244.50
Canny	79.75
Moses McDaniel	797.00
Nick Smith	117.30
Oosaway	286.00
Targeechy	6.00
Cunseenee	323.00
Cabbage	142.50
Choocooa	80.00
Fodder	174.00
Owl Murphy	185.00
Tocoo	612.50
Archibald Murphey	396.00
Ahnilla	118.00
Standing Deer	309.00
Teekatoska	10.00
Johnson Reese	425.00

James Foster	$ 1,744.00
Taana Rogers	-----------
James Hare	476.00
Little Doctor	140.00
Jewnahaka	209.50
Toosawallata	540.50
Nancy Timberlake	117.00
Aggy Foster	290.00
Betsey Section	153.50
Ahweeoosheelka	109.00
Alfred Ellage	162.00
Young Deer	243.00
Charles Timberlake	74.00
Tacahga	666.50
William Reese	327.50
Eahma	60.00
Benjamin Timberlake	515.00
Jack Foster	130.00
Joseph Vann	29,997.10
Sicgeeskee	175.00
Allen Batley	1,283.77
Caneta	224.00
George Field	247.00
David Wilcoxson	233.96
Tecahma	408.00
Males Fields	3,476.50
John R. Blythe	1,247.50
Stake	192.00
William Blythe	303.50
Cahtquaska	130.00
Mose Pathkiller	235.50
Tooenonee	359.00
Pegga waters	372.96 1/8
Red Bird	313.00
Betsy	141.50
Chheosa	523.00
Tocanawaska	61.00
Little Drowningbear	220.00
Big Jim	273.00
Lying Fields	232.50
Calonleska	116.00
Caheeca	1,079.50
Dry	617.00

Cropgrass	$	838.00
Roinannose Johnson		650.00
War Killer		50.00
James Brown		1,579.00
Nose		707.00
Wallee Rotley		188.94
Little Jenny		60.00
William Reed		499.50
Nelly		570.00
Uhaka		338.00
John Poor		221.00
Hunter		106.00
Nathanial Wofford		1,744.75
Corn Tassel		18.50
Oota		553.00
Lizza Batley		78.00
Ellis		106.00
Perry		603.25
Deer Comet		171.00
Mary Ann Howel		135.00
Johnson Murphy		423.00
Andrew Ross		8,875.00
Cloud		160.00
Susan Jane Halin		396.00
Standbefore		71.50
David McLaughlan		233.00
Hawk		40.00
Andrew McLaughlan		284.50
Theodore Shulz, Treasurer & c.		7,055.00
Whirlwind and Nelly		76.50
Margaret Lassly		1,345.00
David Downing		171.00
Echieleher		316.00
Sleeping Robbitt		974.00
Fichancy		604.00
William Williams		6,399.00
Chnalooka		503.50
Lewis Helterbrand		855.00
Black Fox		362.00
Oowayaatoo		76.00
Betsey Spaniard		259.50
Cotaquaskee		61.00
John Spaniard		40.00

Name	Amount
Black Fox	$ 126.00
Heanna	555.00
Mariah Mulkey	1,213.00
Basa Baldridge	887.00
Susannah Otterlifter	193.00
Drowning Bear	3,844.00
Foonanauler	388.50
Bill Dutch	70.00
Woman Killer	238.50
John Harris	642.00
Setting Down	86.00
Watter	320.00
Trotting Wolf	117.00
SawNee	56.00
John Noyeka	61.00
Unchawa	706.00
Young Turkey	34.00
James Gooden	245.00
Silver Jack	65.00
Flea	67.00
Unaketehe	464.50
Conequeoqua	358.00
Pecker Wood	375.00
Jack Baldridge	154.00
Osteelee	30.00
Thomas Foreman	2,960.00
Sarah Dennis	170.00
Captain Hare Conrad	2,231.00
John Benge	2,283.90
Thomas Manning	1,259.50
Rising Fawn	205.00
Charles Manning	557.50
Eight Killer	42.00
Richard Sanders	749.00
John Fox Baldridge	1,456.75
Betsey Walker	1,640.00
Robert Benge	563.50
Richard Foreman	962.25
Green F. Baldridge	250.30
Archa Campbell	1,114.00
Ezekiel West	87.50
Widow Battlinggourd	1,266.50
Old Fields	1,427.83 3/4

Kayhina	$ 599.75
Gourd	30.00
Ailsey Eldridge	4,562.50
Kulste's Orphans	296.40
Nathan Hicks	2,585.20
Jesse Hicks	1,139.00
Archibald Path Killeer	726.00
Alexander Brown	657.90
William Blythe, Senior	13,780.00
Glue	330.25
Richard Fields	234.00
Unnohu	170.00
James V. Fields	220.00
Dick Doublehead	289.50
Ned Bark	724.00
George Fields	1,563.00
Lewis Bark	172.50
Ezekiel Fields	1,893.50
Sarah Fields	214.50
John Fields	809.94
Eskalo	296.75
Willis Fields	135.00
Tuluskee	338.00
Glover Thornton	935.00
David Vann	7,075.40
Jacob Seabolt	79.00
Toonanala	248.50
David Taylor	1,872.50
Daniel Davis	8,506.75
Little Archa Scraper	1,213.50
James Vann	1,556.00
Tom SooaKilla	536.55
Betsey	106.50
Bread Cutter	172.00
TeloaPath Killa	139.00
Dick Taylor	7,542.40
Sally	120.50
James Daniel	10,483.50
Adam Seabolt	348.50
David Bell	1,509.00
Betsey Goins	348.50
Archa Fields	1,598.00
Wilson Nevins	2,308.00

Name	Amount
Samuel Foreman	$ 1,667.80
Jeffrey Beck	1,580.00
John Seabolt	1,513.40
Joseph Beck	726.25
Charles F. Foreman	2,893.00
William Lassley	4,954.36
Richard Foreman	521.44
Levi B. Jones	577.00
William McBridge	631.00
John L. Yarnell	1,604.00
T. Gardenhire	2,724.50
Thomas Bigby	519.00
Joseph Crutchfield	13,369.20
Wily Bigby	340.75
Charles Reese	3,073.50
James Bigby	1,843.00
George Harlin	405.00
John S. Marsh	207.50
Isaac Childress	507.50
Nancy Bushy Head	412.62
Mush	250.00
Jack Foreman	511.08
Little Nelly	269.00
Betsey Candy	611.50
Little Nelly's Granddaughter	151.50
Ruth Kowee	280.00
Sleeping Rabbit	209.50
Kukaleeskee	87.00
Dick Doublehead & son	66.18 2/4
Chusqueluntee	149.75
Rattlegourd	214.25
Telakee	20.00
Gayahnah	199.25
Pheasant	24.00
Maahchee	158.50
Daniel B. Hopkins	292.30
Jonas Woodcock	263.00
Mike Walters	452.20
Tomsilalunkee	145.00
Tanchulana	28.00
Coolahtah	190.75
Dickson Price	624.00
Sal	50.00

Ullateeskee	$	52.00
Tom Cook		246.00
Ezekiel Rogers		478.60
Coughloonee		209.25
Cheenoika		45.25
James Pettit		3,406.00
Deer In The Water		30.00
Caiastago		144.50
Henry Seabolt		1,114.50
Clustomer		382.25
Susannah		193.50
Howling Wolf		137.50
Tarcheechy		547.00
Kaneeca		51.00
Jefferson Hair		258.75
JoSkuntake		123.00
W. Blythe and Ira Goddard		2,393.00
Sullee		357.25
Olla Crittenden		205.00
Chicken		155.00
Too Kor		93.00
Susan Peacock		272.75
Jack Leach		230.00
Dave Scunti		65.00
Toothcha		72.50
Pipes		255.75
George Drumgould		135.00
Wagon Crabgrass		275.75
Wolf Murphy		332.00
Jim Crabgrass		138.50
Tesukawa		68.00
Owl		20.00
Overtaker		515.00
Oolahoota		178.50
Sally		20.00
Alsey Smith		92.00
Long Shell Turtle		335.50
Tieskee fields		502.75
George Going Snake		207.00
Johnson Fields		510.00
Tom Going Snake		127.50
John Boston		233.00
Enatauna		268.20

John Riley	$ 10,155.00
Tecatoca	180.50
Philip Inlow	330.00
Tallgoluntee	123.00
Edward Beck	----------
Orchoteesta	103.50
Ootasaata, or Bend About	354.10
Four Killer	167.50
Tesaguess	829.50
Ailsey Crittenden	222.50
George Cherokee	92.00
Fence Maker	210.00
Caty Butler, (Heir of Old Cherokee)	266.00
Bench Leg	319.50
Old Bark	69.00
Green Leaf	129.75
Jackson Luwaja	43.00
Tucksawanne	97.25
Round	10.00
Lightning Bug	108.00
Katuskee	122.00
Hornet	133.00
Bull Frog	166.00
Crickett	56.00
Tesateskee	110.00
Long Charles	210.00
George Owens, Sr.	388.50
George Owens, Jr.	208.00
Polly Murphy	103.50
Johnny Wayne	190.00
Rattler	68.00
Archy Scott	35.00
Thomas Luwaga	120.00
Betsy Luwaga	246.50
Lonne Cowey	138.00
Tenapin	128.00
Katy	60.00
Tail	20.00
George and Apolly	132.00
Lewaga	84.00
Tiesky	44.00
Jack	70.00
Johnson	46.00

Cut Throat	$ 58.00
Shot Pouch	20.00
Cuts By	36.00
Cross Cut Saw	210.00
Ned	78.00
Tenapin's Wife and Heirs	80.50
Joe Chuck	426.50
George	301.00
John Wayne, or Tequanny	361.50
Chicken	146.00
Watcheesee	283.00
Six Killer	143.50
Connaiusky	46.00
Sam Watcheesee	189.00
Wally, an old woman	122.20
Chinequah	69.00
Chewlixa	197.50
Enetah	54.00
Sinchekiller	77.50
Yeisussta	91.00
Goose	52.50
Jake's Widow	31.50
Wilson, a boy	13.50
Soft Mush	21.00
John Wayne	406.00
Chewheluhee	107.50
Whip Lash	52.00
Kianna	157.00
Hog Shooter	151.00
John Christie	558.00
Caty	37.50
Johnson	125.50
John Lige's Wife	10.00
Costalofty	154.00
George	58.00
Chewnewaka	250.00
Chenequa	63.00
The Owl	73.00
Cousehela	280.50
John Towie	72.00
Sam Owl	64.00
The Axe	135.50
Eleconake	40.50

Oskelela	$ 75.50
Consalatah, or George Bear Meat	68.00
Tiesta	126.00
Young Wolf	138.50
Auseena	78.50
Jesse Christie	29.00
Will, an old man	249.75
Ned Christie	1,166.75
Kanesa	93.87 ½
Tauntuskey	159.00
Sweet Water	543.50
Chewtoni, or Ragged Man	261.50
John Wickliff	516.62 ½
Henry Smith	254.75
John Love	1,812.75
Sarah Smith	254.75
John Timpson	1,505.70
Sally Smith	1,242.87 ½
Telasculta, or Ball Sticks	205.00
Sahkenah, Wife of Grasshopper	226.50
Pumpkin Vine	209.00
Concheesta	5.00
Jugg	40.50
Woman Holder	112.75
Chatowwee	78.00
Keuchee	155.50
Little Smoke	157.50
Yoxah, Daughter of Sitawakee	98.00
Allena, Son of Ned Christie	157.00
Wilson	177.00
Nancy Hawkins	311.50
James Hawkins	300.00
Locust	99.00
Cultaclanah	42.00
Taconqualoske	194.75
Sally Begaw	199.50
Nancy Bullet	172.50
Buck Bear Paw	69.00
Old Bear Paw	216.00
Tom Bear Paw, or Big Meat	62.50
John Tucker	55.00
Andrew Kell and Wife	447.55
Annakee	49.00

Jessey Skilley	$ 25.37 ½
War Club	126.45
John Hawkins	31.00
Tooney	101.50
Charley Jones	139.50
Checatowista	52.00
Techexkah, or Cropper	144.75
Joseph Locust	68.25
Nameconaha	131.25
Coneskly	131.25
Wenenohe	132.00
Arkaluke	23.00
Saluwaje, or Fodder	129.75
Skilla, or Cunning Witch	80.25
Obediah	30.00
Cotaquaskey, or Sunday Fodder	61.00
Nickotoy (a woman)	44.00
Tickcawkeeka	67.75
James Blythe and Wife	454.00
Chunehut, or Little John	193.25
Jackson	213.50
Margaret Ann Hawks	514.25
John Welch	2,205.00
Rosey Hawkins	162.06 1/4
Jehualee, (a woman)	102.25
Cullacholata	86.00
Ollika	258.75
Oleta	71.25
Atowhee	19.25
Chalataskee	141.25
Gideon T. Morris and Wife	2,407.25
Path Killer	61.00
Tecassanaga	174.75
Saluwayha	41.00
Heirs of Little Will	188.00
Ginney	135.75
Culsowwee	52.50
Nake, (a woman)	108.00
Cuttiee, do.	67.50
Walla, do.	125.50
Chewlowee	61.00
Susan Little Deer	188.50
Wacheechee	696.00

Oolaay, (5 ft. high, 23 years old)	$ 58.00
Jenny Daniel	106.00
Aunilla, (a woman)	96.25
Dun Bean	21.00
Sinka, or Mink, (6 ft. high)	154.00
Walla, (a woman 50 years old)	63.00
Toonenolla	14.00
Mose Parch Corn Flour	118.25
Sarah, (English George's Wife)	23.50
Parch Corn Flour	245.50
Chewanannee	279.00
Johnny Wayne, (5 ft. high)	89.37 ½
Linkakoo, or Johnny Hog	81.00
Lucy, (a widow woman)	210.00
Caty, do. do.	43.00
Nancy, do. do.	157.00
Cary, (50 years old)	198.25
Chicksuttahee	10.00
Locust, (40 years old)	60.25
Sahtahkah, or Harvey	61.00
Welah	337.50
Junaluska	174.75
Wahhegahannah, or Going Wolf	57.50
Ahmucatah	194.50
Wakahguatchia	151.50
Taconcah, or Flute	80.00
Double Potts sitting	105.25
Jake Welake	40.00
Suwannah	148.00
Cuttiaah, (a woman)	44.00
Noonatalwyah	37.00
Cunnanatuska, (a woman)	48.50
Sutallah	85.00
Inuah, (a woman)	141.12 ½
Dave	91.76
Standing Dew	51.00
Connachewayah	136.25
Ooncheestanelah	50.62 ½
Culsutahee, (Chief of Connehetu town0	581.37 ½
Scohah	202.50
Jekah	341.75
Tonneah	109.50
Connelukahee	125.00

Salolaaneta	$ 117.00
Old Coon, (60 years old)	126.50
Caty, (50 years old)	198.25
Chicksuttahee	10.00
Locust, (40 years old)	60.25
Sahtahkah, or Harvey	61.00
Welah	337.50
Junaluska	174.75
Wahhegahannah, or Going Wolf	57.50
Ahmucatah	194.50
Wakahguatchia	151.50
Taconcah, or Flute	80.00
Do ble Potts Sitting	105.25
Jakewelake	40.00
Suwannah	148.00
Cuttiaah, (a woman)	44.00
Noonatalawyah	37.00
Cunnanatuska, (a woman)	48.50
Sutallah	85.00
Inquah, (a woman)	141.12 ½
Dave	91.75
Standing Deer	51.00
Connachewayah	136.25
Ooncheestanelah	50.62 ½
Culsuttahee, (Chief of Connehetu Town)	581.37 ½
Scohah	202.50
Jekah	341.75
Tonneah	109.50
Connelukahee	125.00
Oochaleetah	111.75
Santah	145.00
Johnston	212.50
George, (Chief of Cherokeee)	351.75
Oosta Lofty	68.75
Tawney, (a woman)	81.75
Alcey	45.00
Chesquayah	69.50
Tickakeeskah	224.75
Atowhee	562.00
Onneelowhee	193.00
Ottolahee	29.00
Alquah	54.25
Cutsuttahee	63.00

Chakyahtakee	$	44.00
Nonatlah		57.50
Ahqyatakee		127.50
Weocistah		127.50
Enolee		72.75
Chewsaualla		47.00
Ooclauotah		110.25
Standing Turkey		221.50
Equitcha		137.50
Chewwachakah		58.72
Sweetwater		191.00
Seuseste, or Key		267.00
Askaquah		149.00
Cheesquah, or Bird		57.00
Coteeskah		147.00
Chewwahchekah		510.00
Wahhayah		133.00
Sawnanah		151.00
Nakah		93.50
Culsuttahee		64.00
Culquotake		51.00
Nancy, an old woman		46.00
Jesse		9.00
Chutaallatah		36.00
John		63.00
Tomaka		57.50
Ahtasuttahee		46.50
Yonawatla, or Bear at Home		5.00
Tesuiska, or Tanner		72.00
Nancy, Mother of Barrow		185.50
Cannlla, or Barrow		620.50
Chewwee		207.00
Oochaswtasah		52.50
Salaxqua		35.00
Keucha		68.00
Annakeeska		68.50
Kogah		112.00
Aqualakah		58.00
Heirs of Chicken Toater		122.50
Enequah		104.25
Wakakoo		167.37 ½
Wayaneeta		62.62 ½

Darkey, or woman	$	305.75
Cnlsutee		190.50
Collawollah		42.50
Nancy, a woman		105.00
Duck, or Keowanna		114.50
Katy		255.00
Nagkaleeska		225.75
Tetonneeska		35.00
Wessah, or Cat		121.50
Pheasant		9.00
Arkaluke		118.00
Oonaseeka		136.00
Conneenateeska		59.00
Tooalah		52.00
Ookeelah		9.50
Toolahlah		196.00
Tuckaneeska		75.00
Tickconnewteeska		91.50
Charley		47.00
July		145.50
Toonowwee		99.00
Caty		90.25
Tom		108.50
Ameahcatoga		8.00
John Walker		66.75
Connaskeeska		27.00
Nacheeah		55.00
Dickey		170.55
Chewaluah		26.00
Oonanutee		46.87. ½
Wahyakakeeska		14.00
Yonahneyeskee		131.00
Consonah		103.00
Tutustee		58.00
Jim		69.00
Johnnie Waynie		64.00
Jinny		43.00
Toultalah		29.00
Egaculla		282.00
Chewtonah		135.00
Ulesconnah		156.75
Telalluhee		107.00
Ancheelah		8.87 ½

Little Will	$ 256.00
Arch, the Preacher	344.00
Kulksan, or Buck	320.50
The Going Panther, Jr.	50.00
Ratler	196.93
Connauseeteeskee	196.50
Teesawleeskee	46.00
Culsowwee	176.75
Little George	24.00
Alltolatitee, (a woman)	164.00
Tahyana	75.00
Lowen	188.25
Little Deer	46.50
Oostenakee	144.00
Ahtowwee	320.00
Taconnawasee	65.50
Ahanlahchenah	81.00
Wahyaheaktoga	140.00
Chusquah	81.00
Tenelseena	24.00
Loen, Jr.	22.00
Ecooah	22.20
Jake	80.00
Anquatakee	115.75
Clantucha	154.00
Winney, a woman	165.00
John Gessen or Gibson	105.50
Becca	59.50
Skittakee	45.75
Jesse	28.00
Tuskageeta	66.00
Tecenneskee	50.50
Path Killer	55.50
Big Tom	59.50
Nelly	224.00
Chulatoga	14.00
Tahyahkee	213.25
Fishing Hawk	65.75
Waitie	66.00
Cheeschaw or Rabbit	109.25
Lewin	217.50
Charley	206.00
Oochella	155.00

Cloud	$ 131.50
Wattee	112.00
Tawleescah	156.50
Betsey, (an old woman)	20.25
Amachanah	53.00
Aneetsah	135.50
nowaltah	76.50
Yonah Waltah	106.00
Esutee	343.50
Tickconseska	243.00
Tickossenake	55.00
Yankee	36.00
The Old Rabbit, (80 years)	146.00
Cularksaw	18.00
Aneetsa	61.50
Olitee	85.00
Ooorah, or Old Trout	73.00
Hog Bite	150.00
Chalowee, son of Hog Bite	83.00
Deer Out of Water	29.00
Arch	187.00
Takah, a woman	89.00
Wahyouska	215.50
Ahyanoolah, (a woman)	92.00
Naqueesah	19.00
Elowee	70.00
Suwaga	26.00
Nickatie	21.00
Shawnee John, or John Ben	111.75
Little Mannia	140.25
Chewauchucker	149.00
The Mad Woman	92.00
Chogo	161.00
Suwaga	112.50.
Chogohee, Wife of Fire	53.50
The Cloud	257.25
Toostoo, or Spring frog	383.87 ½
Jane Crier	195.25
All Bones	186.00
Tonnoonie, 45 years old	191.50
Tetenteeska, or Dull Hoe	164.62 1/4
Wakey, (Wolf's Wife)	157.25
Otanneeska	141.12 ½

Cheestachee, or Mouse	$ 76.00
Ooacheesta	90.75
Persimmon Toater	141.00
Nakey, daughter of Shawnee John	77.00
Nancy, or Nancy Green	71.50
Conanthestha, (Mouse's daughter)	4.00
Cuttank, so of Nakey)	20.25
Nakee, (Wolf's old wife)	152.00
Jane Walker	221.50.
Tootenchettah, and daughter Sally	229.00
Chickooe	130.00
Atowee, an old man	56.00
Toonanallah, or Arch	281.75
Osquinney, a woman	120.75
Ahyayoh	211.50
Oohaloga, or Bark	27.50
Chemtogagakah, or Flat Face	62.50
Checkanecka, or Otter Lifter	68.25
Betsey, an old woman	95.50
Ball Town George, and Wakah	458.00
Wally, sister of Ball Town George	124.50
Cuttee, or Toonie	134.00
John Lige	34.00
John Davis	28.50
Chewtasalah	100.00
Peckewood	235.75
Nancy	176.00
Toowattee, a woman	18.00
Anneah, (Bird's Widow)	170.50
Katy Bird	183.00
Chinlah	213.50
Wassah, or Mose	21.00
Atawkeesky, a Big Walker	35.00
Fence Maker	232.00
Johnson Muskrat and Wife	152.00
Coloneeske	184.00
Arch the Preacher	229.50
Cahcowee, or Chewla Jim	447.25
Chayuka, or Big Charley	117.00
Juquah	69.00
Stinson, a boy	31.00
Big John	10.00
Tooney, an old woman	219.50

Sapsucker	$ 37.00
John Hood	98.00
Amoscosita, or Tom	50.00
Santoola	250.50
Connacatoga	143.00
Toniah	151.50
Chucheah	88.50
Takah, the Glass Widow	139.00
Jinny (Big Charley's Wife)	140.50
Atoolahee	39.00
Johnny Ess, or John George	10.00
Jonathan England	1,198.25
Sam Cowfeeder	205.00
Oochalatah, or Ned Freeman	115.00
Ailsey	96.00
Dick Downing	1,032.50
Celia Silversmith and Husband	416.50
Little Betsey	211.50
Jack Downing	732.25
Oesuttee	194.75
Colechee	36.50
John Tucker	159.25
Anecosteah	131.00
Mickochee	84.50
Isaac Tucker	66.00
Oolahnahee	54.50
Josawattah	70.25
Johnson Shavehead	64.00
Aginah, a woman	142.00
Nahnah, or Davy Sier	152.00
Nickojack	202.50
Kenah, or Keaner	218.75
Echacha	297.00
Chegatekahwah	115.00
Susan Silversmith	44.75
Jackson Muskrat	204.50
Tuttiah (a woman)	44.50
Big Mouth	42.00
Youaquah	106.25
Johnson Robins and Wife	70.50
Johnny Wayne and Wife	53.00
Caneetahtah	97.50
Cohhahhayetake	66.50

Jim Charles	$	68.50
Ahyowah		173.00
Ootiah		38.00
Colachee, a woman		61.00
Chualaquesska		179.25
Suwaja		32.50
Jack Rabbit		372.00
Darkery, woman		190.37 ½
Estoeagee		8.50
Halla (Standing Turkey)		63.00
Nickochee and Annakee		223.25
Chnechee, or Little Jim		35.00
John Snail		78.00
Chasolah		61.00
Jim Downing		211.50
Chewaloaga		123.75
Jack Downing		195.00
Toowatah, an old woman		40.00
Satagah		412.50
Amuatah		330.50
Cheeneetacah, or Stump		194.25
Yanaquah		108.00
Costiah		81.00
Costanakoo		412.00
Sally		136.50
Wahchetcher		260.00
Stawanah		75.00
Cheenohaka		36.50
Kitajeeska		186.00
Johnson Kitajeeska		86.50
Aneneetooyah		79.75
Arch		77.50
Culsawwee		152.87 ½
Wassah, or Cat		308.00
Wallatsah		26.00
Oowayyasaltah		45.00
Oocdhastosah		681.50
Wilsultalahee		272.50
Sutteach		97.00
Wahsa		61.00
Nancy		148.25
Charley Downing		65.62 ½
Cowanesta		134.50

Conseehah	$	157.75
Alaqueeskah		43.00
Whalarchy		61.50
She Bat		235.50
Rattler, or Will Otter		297.50
Wahhalah, or Eagle		197.00
Connesuttah		102.00
Long Will		46.00
Awee (a woman)		37.00
Johnson		37.00
Tickkanootesahha		44.00
Muskrat		366.00
John Muskrat		617.00
Will		237.25
Ananakatahee		174.25
Ned Muskrat		139.50
Johnson Muskrat		153.00
Chochuck		96.00
Hannah Perry		----------
D. M. Harlin		----------
S. Craig and Wife		----------
Susan J. Perry		----------
Lydia		----------
Johnson Kagg, or Roberts and wife Caty		76.00
Wakee, or Peggy		30.00
Sally Justice		445.00
Takey Justice		163.00
Joseph Coody		----------
Ketcher Smith		----------
Big Road		----------
Turtle		----------
Chickasaw		----------
Nancy		----------
Malikah Parris		201.00
William Coleman		----------
Jim Soap		----------
Charles Tobacco Pouch		----------
Little Land		----------
Ellick		----------
John and Sally Miller		----------
Lack Langley		60.00
Tarchechee Terrill		292.50
Ahtahlahlee		----------

Name	Amount
Sally, John's Wife	$ 60.00
Peggy	----------
James Madison	47.00
Cattelohuh	
Sally	
David Miller	
Elijah	
William L. Holt	
Robert B. Vann	
Eliza Campbell	
Dorcas Sanders	
Quatee, Bearhead's Wife	
Cheuka, Widow of Horn	
Culsti, one of the Heirs of Horn	
Chuskoeeska, one of the Heirs of Horn	
Lydia, One of the Heirs of Horn	
George Downing	
George, John, Owayni, and Nancy, Heirs of Ketiah	84.50
Cooesster	
Nancy Baldridge	
Charles Smith	
Stooping George	59.50
Heirs of Ned Keener, deceased	156.00
Amawhuah	74.00
Hog Shooter, Wife and Children	104.00
Sampson Dick	136.00
Heirs of Celia Tucker	304.00
Chouencah, (a woman)	91.00
Culstiah	837.75 ½
Coohuitah	66.00
Martin D. Cheek	362.00
Heirs of Dreadful Water	252.00
Chuhee	50.00
Tyeaskey	98.00
Aka McPherson	60.00
Pheasant	84.00
Young Turkey	88.00
John Kell	150.00
Susan McClure	37.00
Polly Wicked	225.00
Peggy Wicked	127.00
John Tidwell	77.00
Heirs of Leecowee	115.00

Sally Thompson	$ 156.00
Heirs of Pretty Woman	110.00
Tarkahyah	60.00
Sapsucker	121.00
Heirs of Nancy	100.00
Chenawah	140.00
Rotten Wood	195.00
Calakah, or Blacksnake	111.00
Claudlalonahaska	---------
Alsa, and one other, name unknown	170.00
Heirs of Jesse Smith	345.00
Susannah Reid	520.00
Heirs of Utsak, deceased	185.00
Agga Old Field's second wife	610.00
Ruth Bowling	274.00
Tying	79.00
Skaga, or Seen	30.00
Sequieleesa	112.00
Archibald McCurty	76.00
Nancy Butler	675.75
James and Peggy, Heirs of John Hill	120.00
Heirs of Calaga	95.00
English Jim	75.00
Skiugah's Heirs	75.00
Chulogguhtah	70.00
Steekatogah	175.00
Heirs of Sam, deceased	25.00
Wattee, a woman	180.00
Chalahkeedhi	
Clem Foster	
Tonneyey Canal	
Nancy of Georgia	
Ahkiula	
Aunee, of Cass County, GA	
Anne Crittenden	
Archil and Ailsey	
Elizabeth Lowry	
Nancy Springston	
Wattee, a woman of Alabama	
Susan McPherson	
Ned Vann	
Claud Three Killer	
Ann Dougherty	
Nancy Butler	

Ulateeska	$
Abigal, Wife of Ketchum	
Yocisey	
Nelly Walker	
Neisa	
Moses	
Lydia Sanders	
Tolucha	
Quati, or Betsey	
Jinney	
Lydia	
Twyeskee	
Nancy	269.00
Heirs of Noonday	
Jane McPherson	
Arch Canoe	
Cheelsta, Widow of Cussowee	272.03 1/8
Little Turtle	197.03 1/8
Walase	
Quaakee, or Waga	
Male, Fluwqueta	
Jack Dry	
Lyzzy McDonald	
Alsey, of Red Clay	
Sakey	
Reuben Daniel	
Heirs of Chuwna	56.00
Kiuka	
Heirs of Flute, deceased	
Lacey	
Grubb, Son of Bear Paw	652.50
Tawney	62.00
Thomas Cordery	
Nancy Hicks	
Snake House	
Nancy Griffin	506.00
John McCullough	276.00
Heirs of William Ratley	
Felix W. Riley	109.00
James Richmond	100.00
Mary Welch	
Michael Halfacre	542.00
Richard Cheek	

Jenny Bark	$
John	
Nancy	
Peggy Grimmet	14.00
Nana	
Peggy and Cuntskee, Heirs, & c.	97.00
Sally	
John Shepherd	
D. S. Bell	434.00
Peggy Quaqua	
Isham Taylor	
Robert G. Anderson	
Booker Cheek	
Betsey Cheek	
Rezin Tharp	
Agga	
Nancy Hughes	186.00
Kayooky, or Bogler	40.00
Eleanor	
Heirs of Henry Vickery, deceased	
Anna	
Jinney Owens	
Turtle	
Kootaha	
Nelika	60.00
Tieeska	
John Duncan	
William Huss	
Nancy Carroll	
Heirs of Davis	87,50
Blossom	35.00
Wootee, a woman	189.00
Tyeskey	98.00
Gritts	15.00
George Wakefield	98.00
Tooka, Sally Bark's Mother	113.00
Olive, a woman	
Crying Woman	134.00
Nancy Field	
Chergauuneesky	254.50
Acooah	174.50
Snal	307.00
Jerry Tucker	97.00

Artowivee	$	298.25
Wahyahaniah		23.00
Sam Artowee		32.62 ½
Tarcheeah		113.00
Keenaanetah		139.50
Ooahwasetee		143.00
Tooyahhulla		34.00
Cannerka, or Grass		43,00
Jim Keener		57.00
Betsey Tucker		56.00
Caty Tucker		62.00
Nancy Grass		211.00
George Blair		1,345.00
Robin Muskrat		523.25
Jenny Tayee		108.87 ½
Cheekeeah		181.00
Nicko Jack		175.00
Jesse Muskrat		188.00
Heirs of Shavehead		172.50
Ookahyahtah		54.50
Chogohee		491.00
Tom Spikebush and Mother		281.00
David England and Wife		3,701.50
Oostutley, a woman		32.50
Equilah, or Eelia Equillah		358.12 ½
Nancy		94.00
Little Nanny		58.00
Sarah		49.00
Celia		134.00
Chinnegue Jones		88.00
John Liga		112.50
Hopping Dick		147.00
Anny, a girl 8 or 9 years		82.00
Oochanhattah		132.75
Satagatah		32.00
Ougeechee		60.00
Lying Fish		77.75
Lizzard		62.00
Kalkeener, or Buck		19.00
Jess Grass		443.50
Tianah		54.00
Keellaoosta		112.00
Young Chicken		334.00

Wywahsatee	$	121.00
Bob Walker		244.00
Caty Walker		725.00
Joseph Walker		303.50
John Walker		250.50
Black Fox and Mother		229.00
Sigeowee		113.00
Charles Buffington		325.00
Jesse Buffington		108.00
Ootagusta		91.00
Wahateches		32.00
John Otsee		66.00
Otsee		98.62 ½
Cornanustee		46.00
Cullalohee		55.00
Betsey Buffington		65.00
James Peak		119.00
Peter a Preacher		563.37 ½
Oocahewa		67.00
Chseellawah		97.50
Wahlayahha		197.00
Ookasquata		62.00
Clickanah		30.00
Cloud, Son of Stroller		122.50
Lheta, a woman		137.00
Woikket		63.00
Stroller		193.00
Cahallatah		51.50
Stamp, or Stump		178.50
Chulseyah		149.00
Cholachuatty		187.00
Wahta		44.00
Yohnawatt		181.00
Lacy, a boy 18 years old		37.50
John Walker's Wife Susan		49.00
Wahheysneka		65.50
Ginuey, a woman		300.00
Connatacharje		65.50
Caaneetah		226.00
Settahnee, a woman		60.50
Settahwakee		687.25
Luka		285.75
Cawcaleeska		219.50

Name	Amount
Tawnalsee	$ 111.00
Big Acorn	93.00
Jake	33.00
Keenahtetee	94.00
Wahtoosata	117.00
Nanny Stroller	43.00
Old Hoe	130.50
Cawnahsole	100.00
Tomacha, a Horse Fly	126.37 ½
Oohullacha	45.00
Oolscosita Smoke	68.50
Clinney	495.00
Wake, Wife of Juggy	85.00
Tiulsenah	1,965.50
Thomas Roper and Wife	473.75
Culahsagesee	136.00
James Wafford	136.00
Heirs of Collasquakey	133.00
Widow Mush Ice	89.25
Geroge Cherokee	204.00
George Owens	45.00
Tieeske	48.00
Jessee Roper and Wife	2,305.25
Tenalawhista	70.00
Toononatatah	471.00
Tittiee	72.62 ½
Cowatageeska	151.25
Dick Christy	172.25
Jack Christy	593.25
James Rapier	295.00
Anny, Wife of Bill Bowling	1,060.50
William Bowling	----------
Cheesanhee	79.50
Alsey	118.50
Caheetee, or Big Lanes	131.50
Ahhetah and Chickeah	190.00
Clansehah	88.50
Buzzard	163.50
Caty, Buzzard's Daughter	96.25
Chewkeeoskey	313.50
Lawlan, or Ooclahnotah	305.00
Chattowee	133.50
Maul Head	22.50

Keeneeteehee	$	75.62 ½
Ahseeniee		80.75
Ooyakee		33.00
Sahtaka		317.37 ½
Callelohee		62.50
Sunday		28.00
Chewnonahah		131.75
Secaulgah		104.00
Tualah		63.50
Keelistoga		266.00
Cancaleeska		88.50
Toosawaltah		134.50.
Chocaoh		193.00
Chewiskee		23.00
David Christie		55.00
Johnson Christie		38.50
Scousah, (Kill Deer)		40.00
Tultiee		91.50
Chickoah		170.50
Pheasant		185.50
Cewanah		46.75
Jack Cold Weather		80.00
Ah Wohalah		117.00
To Chuck		176.00
Tahchahsa		73.50
Arch Scott		99.50
George Owens		214.50
Bear Paco		1,110.37 ½
Robin Rowena		39.50
Satoolataney		86.50
Oan kah		55.00
Cheesloquillannah		497.37 ½
Culchusta		141.75
Chuelstilla		28.00
Watatooah		10.50
Punk		104.00
Jack Kill deer		101.00
Nanny Old Woman		123.00
Nickatill		63.00
The Old Horse, or John sige		143.00
Big Nedd		56.00
Sultaltataha		101.00
Sesonnahee, or Jim Spears		214.00

Name	Amount
Toloka	$ 27.00
Old Otter	111.12 ½
Callelekee	158.00
Sulsah and Wife	304.75
Heirs of Aonankate	317.00
Elijah Hicks	2,852.50
Waddee	365.00
Six Killer	598.00
Crying Wolf	536.00
Heirs of Nelly Six Killer	458.00
E. George	50.00
Fool Peter	382.00
Walter Hunter	232.50
Crane Eater	245.00
Dahunaula	228.00
Gahdo Yah	203.00
Shut Door	552.50
Chicken	165.00
Little Archy	120.00
Lizzy Shooboot	692.50
Little Jimmy Crittendon	325.00
Little Sally	184.00
John A. Bill and Joseph Linch	308.00
Pheasant	131.00
Cheeosa	144.00
Tahkaya	147.00
Kahhena Betsey and Dorcas	129.00
Alexander McCoy, a minor	181.00
Richard Ratcliff, Senior	
Nancy	117.25
John Gunter, Jr. and Sr.	11,041.91
Chawangah chesholm	
Betsey Hair	
Nelly Downing	
Ailsey whortleberry	
Sarah Woodward	56.00
Nake, Nitts Wife	
Anley Fields	
Lydia Griffin	
Barney Hughes	
Sinda McDonald	
Nelly Starr	
Aggy McDonald	

Gahlung Skahlo	$
Chawagh Crabgrass	
Sally Tesateske	
Oastoanah	123.00
Arney Tomorrow	
Cahtung Wahlee	
Betsy Caun	
Jesse Murphy	
Cheooe Crittenden	
Heirs of N. D. Scales	2,000.00
Laugh at Mush	120.00
Crying Snake	
John Waine	233.50
Benjamin Downing	287.00
Overseer	70.00
Samuel Terrett	671.00
Ezekiel Drowning Bear	39.00
Heirs of Swimmer	141.00
Brice Martin	963.00
Oosowwee	30.00
Sally	108.00
Walletah	200.50
Chowyouka	56.00
Chewajeeska	44.00
Oatacough	48.00
Chichkeah	39.00
Stop Drowning Bear	349.50
Cinecowhee	50.00
Rising Fawn	94.75
George Blackwood	120.00
Pigeon	146.50
Man Striker	15.00
Dirt Seller	45.00
Lockina	123.00
Oatie	115.00
Cumberland	595.00
Wauldah	67.00
Hukleberry and Wife	68.50
James Landrum, Jr.	97.00
John Bagg	106.00
Calonahskee	90.00
Katchee	324.00
Uretta (Wife of Walking Wolf)	155.00

Jack Wills	$	60.00
Cold Boy		131.00
Swimmer		208.00
Nancy Daldridge		25.00
Nelly McDaniel		94.00
Christina Mastin		183.00
Nelly Martin, (Sam's Wife)		197.00
Robert B. Vann		3,000.00
Collard		126.00
John Collard		32.00
Tanapin		174.00
Weavel		109.00
Peggy		66.00
Buckeye		300.50
Felix Arthur		684.00
Richard Henson		310.00
Alsey Ketchum		144.50
Betsey, Widow of Chueska		260.00
John Blacksmith		30.00
Jake, or Culseegeesku		199.00
Hog, or Beauth		155.00
Edward Edwrds and Wife		348.00
Quatie Murphy		103.33 1/3
Samuel Nellums		57.00
Sarah Hawkins		
Chicken Snake		115.00
Negoodahye		
Thomas Fields		320.00
Andrew Miller's Heirs		
Anna Elwee's Wife		
Leaf		
Bishop		500.50
Tseloarahsee		
Tachee Pheasant		
Sitting Down		
Chickasaw		
Quatie, (John Fish's Wife)		
John McIntosh		
Silas Choate		123.00
Nelly		
Nancy		
Jinny		
Sally Rabbit		

Charles Timberlake and Wife	$ 139.00
Ground Hog	
James Landrum, Sr.	1,993.00
Charles E. Landrum	654.00
Mary Miller	
Sour Mush, or Hawkins	
Darky Mills	
Ailsey Moore	
Tsahwahagah	
Nanny	
Nelly Dirt Seller	
Sam, of Dirt Town	
Coffee and Wife	
Jesse Murphy	
Ailsey	
rana McDaniel	
Nancy Miller	
John Brown, Jr.	52.50
Lydia and Ailsey Kitchum	
Archille	
Jane Beamer	
Ailsey, of Etowa	
Duck, of Wills Valley	
Tallasensa	
Standing Fence	
Gilly Rackley	86.00
Lydia Kitchum	
Rope Lowry	152.00
Elizabeth Weary	
Katty Rabbit	229.00
Sour Mush	
Stop, or Mealy Mouth	129.50
Corn Tassell	306.00
Lucy	113.50
Martin Downing	223.00
James Deer Head	
Lydia Mush	
Celia Baldridge	
Andrew Coward and Wife	1,363.87 ½
Betsy Gourd	
Corn Silk and Wife	
Martin Kilsewee	

Tucksee	$
Martin Davis	
Coleman Davis	575.00
Lorenza D. Davis	535.00
Big Dollar	487.00
Jim Mankiller	
Sarah Sanders	
Ailsey	
Teana Big Dollar	
Kotiah	
James ellack	
Tucker's Heirs	
George Hughes	280.00
Sally Murphy	166.00
Lizzy	358.81 1/4
Nelly Sides	64.00
John Sidney	
Leaf, of Creek Path	
David Night Killer	
Skilly	
Lizzy Dwoning	
Nelly Sides	
David Mankiller	
Hester Graves	43.00
John Bean	
Margaret Bean	1,804.00
Caleb Starr Bean	665.00
Tom Boots	64.00
Rising, or Jesse, (orphan)	314.20
John Potatio	40.00
Towney	190.00
George	55.00
Pretty Woman, a man	185.50
Lydia Fields	101.00
Aqullah	
Daniel A. Perdu	
Skitley	
Path Killer	
Jinny Witch	
David	
Nancy Pheasant	
Nancy Stop	
Betsey Brown	

Tesenahsah	$
Oowahletah	
Tsalahtake	
Towentaaska	
Adaleeskee	
Chasaltee Guess	
Abalam Hillin	3,050.00
Joseph Elliott	3,440.00
Josiah Elliott	1,572.00
David Elliott	708.75
Eldridge Vaughn	292.50
Winford Elliott	774.00
Ame Rackley	106.77
Knight Killer	300.00
Toonah	98.83 ½
Wakey	98.83 ½
Peggy	
Turkey	
Towney	98.83 ½
Jinney, John Love's Old Wife)	941.00
Sally Bark	2,020.00
Jinney Witch	10.00
Nelly, George Saunders' Mother	172.00
Tesa guess	100.00
John Fish	59.00
Robertson Brown	615.00
Terrapin Head, (carrac)	1,000.00
Takey	314.66 ½
Aka	112.00
Martha Dragging Canee	580.00
Cowtawnee	314.66 2/3
Owoteshhe	314.66 2/3
Coming Deer	66.00
Cahnahokah, or Grass	65.00
The Panther	67.00
Katy	40.00
Cullah Quesaaw	85.00
Segowee	69.00
Board of Baptist Missions	4,144.00
Abigail Ketcher	
Harry Coalson	36.00
Thompson, Peggy, and Joe	33.71
N. B. Hyatt's Estate, (deceased)	2,459.00

David and William Reid	$	697.00
Ootehee		
T. Jefferson Pack		606.00
John Riley & Company		392.00
Ootihee		
Nelly		
Betsey		
Lucy Crittenden		
Sarah Thompson		
Heirs of Mary Mankiller		90.00
William Crittenden		
Thomas Smith's Heirs		177.87 ½
Richard Carey		120.00
Lucinda Hicks		
Rachael Brownlow		
Katy Bigby		
Melvina McGhee		
Nelly smith		
Takanaeeska		
Red Bird		874.00
Jackson Soap		
Nancy		
Wild Cat		
Eleanor Pigeon		30.00
Ge About		
Cueeste		
Jesse Owens		
Lucretia Foreman		
Walter Downing		
Robert T. Hanks		
Jack M. Teer		
Suwaka		213.00
Heirs of Fox Fields		590.00
Leaf of Doublehead		219.00
Susanna McDaniel		
Robin		
Bullet Eye		405.50
Rachel Baldridge		
Young Panther		201.50
Ailsey		
Kate Carey		
Oolootsa		
Archibald Foreman		196.00
E.F. Phillips		

James C. Foreman	$
Thomas Tuwaga	
Nancy Swan	
William S. Coody	
Taka Swan	91.12 ½
Choweyonka	
Jack Crittenden	
Toona	
Nelly Fuchalukah	
Olly Baldridge	
Techageesa	
Lizza Drowning Bear	
Huckleberry	
Aka Quaua	174.50
Richard Walker's Heirs	500.00
David Welch	100.00
Bald Head	
Uncenti	
John H. Storer	593.00
George Ward	1,259.00
Charles Duncan	179.00
E. Wilson's Widow	269.00
Syah	
George W. Parris	136.00
Wannakee	
William Green	

Bibliography

Johnson, Steven L. *Guide to American Indian Documents in the Congressional Series, 1817-1899*. Clearwater Pub. Co. Inc. New York and Paris. [1977] p. 62. No. 107. SD 277, 25-3, v5, 100pp. [342]. NARA Microfiche. Original Data.

Trail of Tears Association, Oklahoma Chapter. *1835 Cherokee Census. Monograph Two*. Trail of Tears Association, Oklahoma Chapter. Park Hill, OK. [2002] pp. 68-88.

Watson, Larry S. *Indian Treaties, 1785 to 1768. B. II -Cherokee*. Based on Charles J. Kappler. Histree. Laguna Hills, CA. [1992] p. 59.

Cherokee Nation. Cherokee Census. [1835]. Micropublication T496, Roll 1. Washington, DC National Archives.

Index:

Abigal, 70,
Acooah, 71,
*Acorn, 16, 21,
*Adair, 10, 11(2), 12(3), 13, 16, 41, 42,
Adaleeskee, 81,
*Adam, 32, 35,
Afanlatee, 15,
*Agga, 71,
Aginah, 65,
Ah Wohalah, 75,
Ahauma, 4,
Ahchotahe, 43,
Ahhetah, 74,
Ahkiula, 69,
AhleeChah, 42,
Ahlula, 8,
Ahmee, 44,
Ahmucatah, 59,
Ahmucatah, 58,
Ahnalahchenah, 62,
Ahnilla, 47,
Ahnonhee, 27,
Ahqyatakee, 60,
Ahseeniee, 75,
Ahtahlahlee, 67,
Ahtasuttahee, 60,
Ahtooeska, 46,
Ahwattee, 12,
Ahweeoosheelka, 48,
Ahyanoolah, 63,
Ahyayoh, 64,
Ahyowah, 66,
*Ailsey, 37, 65, 69, 79(2), 80, 82,
Aka, 6, 45, 81,
Akelineka, 4,
Ala, 14,
Alaqueeskah, 67,
Alberd, vii,
*Alberty, 35,
Alcy(ey), 44, 59,
Alequah, 59,

Alexander, 14,
*All Bones, 38, 63,
Allena, 56,
Allgone, 37,
Allkeenah, 1,
Alltolatitee, 62,
Alnehna, 18,
Alsa, 14, 69,
Alsey, 39, 70, 74,
Alumn, 20,
Amachanah, 63,
Amaly, 19,
Amatuskah, 20,
Amawhuah, 68,
Ameahcatoga, 61,
Amertoyehah, 11,
Amoscosita, 65,
Amuatah, 66,
Anahalee, 29,
Ananakatahee, 67,
Ancheelah, 61,
Anderson, 71,
Anecosteah, 65,
Aneetsa(h), 63(2),
Aneneetooyah, 66,
Anianka, 9,
Anley, 40,
Anna, 8, 37, 71,
Annakee, 56, 66,
Annakeeska, 60,
*Annawake, 46,
Anneah, 64,
Annennetto, 5,
*Anney(y), 35, 72,
*Anny, 74,
Anquatakee, 62,
Anuhahee, 25,
Aonankate, 76,
Aqualakah, 60,
Aqullah, 80,
*Arch, 3, 33, 62, 63, 64(2), 66,
Archil, 69,
Archilla, 79,

Arkaluke, 57, 61,
Arlee(y), 33, 37,
*Arnold, 3, 8,
Arquaria, 31,
Arquoneeska, 28,
Arseekeeta, 45,
Arthur, 78,
Artowa, 32,
Artowee, 72,
Artowivee, 72,
Ashes, 43,
Askaquah, 60,
Askee, 41,
Assulita, 11,
Astahuah, 11,
Astowkee, 15,
Atawa, 24,
Atawhee, 15,
Atawkeesky, 64,
Atawlah, 8,
Atoolahee, 65,
Atowee, 64,
Atowhee, 59,
Atowhee, 57,
Atowwee, 62,
Augoonaneechee, 37,
*Augusta, xi,
Auley, 18,
Aunee, 69,
Aunilla, 58,
Auqua, 47,
Auseena, 56,
Awee, 67,
Awnerly, 33,
Ayankee, 63,
*Back Bone, 42, 45,
*Bag(g), 6, 77,
Baily, 25,
Bain Frog, 46,
Bald Head, 83,
Baldnage, 79,
*Baldridge, 1, 2, 17, 24, 41, 44, 50(4), 68, 82, 83,

*Ball Sticks, 56,
Barb, vi,
Barclay, v,
Bark Floot, 29,
*Bark, 24, 51, 64(2), 71(2), 81,
Barnes, 18,
*Barraw, 16,
Barrow, 14, 60(2),
Barrowtenna, 19,
Batley, 48, 49,
Batt, 42,
*Beamer, 40, 47, 79,
*Bean, 22, 30, 32, 58, 80(3),
*Beanstick, 44,
*Bear, 24,
*Bear at Home, 60,
*Bear Paw, 33, 39, 42, 56(2), 70,
Bear Head(s), 1, 42, 68,
*Bear Meat, 11, 12, 56,
*Bear Paw, 33, 39, 42, 56(2), 70,
Bear Ponch, 26,
Bear Stick, 16,
Beauth, 78,
*Beaver Tail, 25,
*Beaver Toater, 30, 40(2),
*Beaver(s), v,
Becca, 62
*Beck, 16, 31, 52(2), 54,
Beemer, 3,
Begaw, 56,
*Bell, vii, viii(2), ix, 2, 9, 21(2), 51, 71,
Bench Leg, 54,
Bend About, 54,
*Benge, 18(2), 23, 50(2),
Bennet(t), 16, 29,
*Berry, 32,
Bete, 11,
*Betsey(sy), 44, 48, 51, 63, 64, 70, 76, 78, 82,
Bevint, 3,
*Big Acorn, 74,
Big Bean, 30,
*Big Bear, 39, 40, 46,
Big Charley, 64, 65,

*Big Coat, 36,
*Big Coon, 11,
*Big Dave, 35(2),
*Big Dollar, 80,
Big Elk, 40,
*Big Field, 21,
Big Head, 39,
*Big Hoe, 18,
*Big Jack, 44,
*Big Jim, 48,
*Big John, 30, 64,
Big Kettle, 6,
Big Lanes, 74,
*Big Meat, 56,
Big Milk, 10,
Big Mouth, 65,
*Big Mush, 25,
Big Nedd, 75,
Big Rising Fawn, 34,
Big Road, 67,
Big Smoke, 37,
Big Tom, 62,
*Bigby, viii, 17, 52(3), 82,
*Bill, 3, 76(2), 82,
*Bird, 20, 28, 37, 45, 60, 64,
Bishop, iii, 78,
*Biter, 22, 27,
Black Beard, 27,
Black Fog, 15,
*Black Fox, 16, 41, 49, 50, 73,
*Black George, 45,
Black Jack, 28,
Blackban, 22,
*Blackbird (Black Bird), 11, 14, 20,
*Blackburn, 1, 43,
Blackman, 3,
Blacksmith, 78,
Blacksnake, 69,
Blackwood, 31, 77,
*Blair, 72,
*Blanket, 34(2), 38,
Blinkey, 38,
*Blossom, 33, 71,

Blinkey, 38,
*Blossom, 33, 71,
Blowjah, 31,
Blue Bird, 17,
*Blue Calf, 29,
*Blythe, 48(2), 51, 53, 57,
Board of Baptist Missions, 81,
Bob, 4,
*Bogg(s), 2, 44,
Bogler, 71,
Boiled Corn, 9,
Boneater, 12,
Bonery, 20,
*Boots, 22, 80,
*Boston,
*Boudinot, 13,
Bow, 20(2),
Bowling, 69, 74(2),
Boy, 21,
Boyd, vi,
Brams, 21,
Brand, 40,
Branham, 4,
*Bread, 13, 47,
*Bread Cutter, 51,
*Brewer, 12(2), 31,
Bright, 27,
*Broom, 42(2),
*Brown, vi, ix(2), xi, 4, 15, 29, 41, 44, 49, 51, 79, 80, 81,
Brownlow, 82,
Bruce, vi,
Brush, 44,
*Brush in the water, 10,
*Buck, 36, 62, 72,
*Buckeye, 78,
*Buckingham & Huntington, xi,
Bud, 22,
*Buffalo(e), 2, 10, 14, 25(2), 27,
Buffaloo Head, 17,
*Buffington, 13, 20, 73(3),
*Bug, 6,
*Bull, 16, 32,

*Bullard, 12,
*Bullet, 56,
Bullet Eye, 82,
*Burns(es), 17, 47,
Burnt Wood, 36,
*Bushyhead, 17(3), 39(4), 41, 52,
*Butler, 7, 17, 54, 69,
*Buzzard, 8, 74(2),
*Byers, iv, viii,
Caaneetah, 73,
*Cabbage, 47,
*Cabin, 18,
Cade, 9, 21,
Cahallatah, 73,
Cahchaseaneesca, 46,
*Cahcowee, 64,
Caheeca, 48,
Caheetee, 74,
Cahnahokah, 81,
Cahnatana, 14,
Cahnawsaska, 44
Cahoogishei, 6,
Cahrahquilta, 44,
Cahskahneehe, 42,
Cahtquaska, 48,
Cahucca, 35,
Caiastago, 53,
Calaga, 69,
Calakah, 69,
Caldwell, iii,
Calenahaaska, 22,
Callelekee, 76
Callelohee, 75,
Calogee, 41,
Calonahskee, 77,
Calonleska, 48,
Camel, 29,
Cameron, 14(2),
*Campbell, 26, 50, 68,
Camron, 24,
Canal, 69,
Canawsawsky, 6,
Cancaleeska, 75,

Caneetahtah, 65,
Caneka, 15,
Canesauayah, 5,
Caneta, 48,
Canlla, 60,
Cannaiusky, 54,
Cannerka, 72,
Cannon, iv, v,
Canny, 47,
*Canoe, 70,
Canotitah, 22,
Canseeme, 43,
Canuesky, 7,
*Carey, 41, 82(2),
Carlooneheskee, 20,
Carr, vi,
Carrac, 81,
*Carroll, 71,
Cart, 14,
*Carter, 2,
Cartoo, 11,
Cartso, 47,
*Cary, 58,
Casguattre, 42,
*Cat, 8, 27, 61, 66,
Cat Fish, 14, 39,
Catageeskee, 15,
Catawbee, 25,
Catayostah, 36,
Catehe, 16,
Catowee, 44,
Catron, 22,
Cattelohuh, 68,
*Caty, 6, 40, 55, 58, 59, 61, 67, 74,
Caun, 77,
Cawcaleeska, 73,
Cawnahsole, 74,
Caynga, 18,
Caytee, 42,
Cekekee, 28,
Cekeookuekee, 28,
Celia, 72,
Chalahkeeehi, 69,

Chalowee, 63,
Chaluski, 37,
Chamberlain, ix,
*Chambers, 16, 17, 25(2),
Chanchee, 27,
Charlaerhee, 24,
*Charles(ey, ie, ly), 1, 3, 7, 28, 32, 33, 34, 42, 61, 62, 66,
Charletehee, 46,
Chasolah, 66,
Chatowwee, 56,
Chattowee, 74,
Chaueska, 7,
Chauhah, 5,
Chayuka, 64,
Cheanwee, 3,
Checatowista, 57,
Checkanecka, 64,
Checooah, 20,
Chee, 23,
Cheeellawah, 73,
Cheeenohgee, 41,
Cheegachawna, 13,
*Cheek, 68, 70, 71(2),
Cheekelteehee, 44,
Cheelie, 43,
Cheelsta, 70,
Cheenahwee, 41,
Cheeneetacah, 66,
Cheenohaka, 66,
Cheenoika, 53,
Cheeosa, 76,
Cheesanhee, 74,
Cheeschw, 62,
Cheesetand, 37,
Cheesloquillannah, 75,
Cheesquah, 60,
Cheestachee, 64,
Cheeusta, 8,
Cheeva, 22,
Chegatekahwah, 65,
Chemtoganakah, 64,
Chenawah, 69,

Chenequa, 55,
Chenoika, 6,
Chenoquah, 5,
Chenuckeva, 38,
Chererconseelee, 46,
Chergauuneesky, 71,
Chernrske, 2,
*Cherokee, 54, 74,
*Chesnut, 45,
Chesquayah, 59,
Chester, ix,
Cheuka, 68,
Chewa, 31,
Chewajeeska, 77,
Chewakika, 33,
Chewaloaga, 66,
Chewaluah, 61,
Chewaluka, 37,
Chewanah, 75,
Chewanannee, 58,
Chewauchucker, 63,
*Chewee, 17, 35,
Chewgahnalilanah, 13,
Chewheluhee, 55,
Chewiskee, 75,
Chewkeeoskey, 74,
Chewla Jim, 64,
Chewlixa, 55,
Chewlowee, 57,
Chewnewaka, 55,
Chewnonahah, 75,
Chewnonner, 38, 53,
Chewsaulle, 60,
Chewtasalah, 64,
Chewtonah, 61,
Chewtoni, 56,
Chewwachakah, 60,
Chewwahchekah, 60,
Chewwee, 60,
Cheyawsee, 29,
Chhemugah, 41,
Chheosa, 48,
Chichkeah, 77,

Chickanaler, 9, 30,
Chickasaw, 67, 78,
Chickea, 45,
Chickeah, 74,
*Chicken, 29, 33, 53, 55, 76,
Chicken Crown, 38,
*Chicken Snake, 34, 44, 78
Chicken Toater, 60,
Chickooe, 64,
Chickoohee, 28,
Chicksatahee, 39,
Chicksuttahe(e), 58, 59,
Chicoleska, 23,
*Chikalela, 42,
Childress, 18, 19, 52,
Chinequah, 55,
Chinlah, 64,
*Chisholm, 47,
Chnalooka, 49,
Chnechee, 66,
Choachuka, 35,
Choate, 25, 78,
Chocaoh, 75,
Chochuck, 67,
Choctaw Killer, 21,
Chogo, 63,
Chogohee, 63, 72,
Choka, 6,
Cholachuatty, 73,
Chooa, 42,
Choocooa, 47,
Chooie, 44,
Choomaheca, 45,
Choonstooeh, 4,
Choonstoostee, 24,
Choosu, 5,
Chopper, 37,
Chouencah, 68,
Chowauqua, 28,
Chowawha, 34,
Chowewka, 45,
Choweyonka, 83,
Chowyouka, 77,

*Christy(ie), 7, 39(2), 55, 56(2), 74(2), 75,
Chualaquesska, 66,
Chualeoka, 47,
Chuc, 46,
Chucheah, 65,
Chucheechee, 44,
*Chuck, 55,
Chuelstilla, 75,
Chueska, 78,
Chuhee, 68,
Chuiheitla, 6,
Chuklahtakee, 60,
Chulacyah, 73,
Chulaskatuhee, 4,
Chulatoga, 62,
Chulogguhtah, 69,
Chuluah, 28,
Chune, 7,
Chunehut, 57,
Chuqualalaqu, 11,
Chusktah, 1,
Chusquah, 62,
Chusqueluntee, 52,
Chutaallatah, 60,
ChutaKah, 22,
Chuwna, 70,
Chyauka, 8,
Cinecowhee, 77,
Clansehah, 74,
Clantucha, 62,
Clapboard, 19,
Claudialonahaska, 69,
Clawyacahnah, 15,
Cleland, 5,
Clickanah, 73,
*Clingon, 17,
Clinney, 74,
Cloaka, 16,
Clohquohlohtoh, 41,
Cloida, 9,
*Cloud, 30, 34, 49, 63, 73,
Clustomer, 53,
Coalson, 81,

*Coate, 35,
Coats, 39(2),
Cock, 11,
Cock Roaster, 40,
*Cockran, 30(2),
*Coffee, 79,
Cogerohyohleeskee, 14,
Cohhahhayetake, 65,
Coker, 29,
Colachee, 66,
Cold Boy, 78,
*Cold Weather, 75,
Cole, 30,
Colechee, 65,
Coleman, 67,
Collaquaskey, 74,
Collard, 78(2),
Collawollah, 61,
Collins, xi, xiii(5), 5,
Coloneeske, 64,
Colostola, 30,.
Coluwee, 39,
Comet, 49,
Coming Deer, 81,
Conanthestha, 64,
Concheesteeche, 24,
Conconah, 61,
Coneenateeska, 61,
Conequeoqua, 50,
Conesawlewah, 23,
Coneskly, 57,
Congolawhattie, 45,
Conlakee, 39,
Conna, 35,
Connacatoga, 65,
Connachewayah, 58, 59,
Connatacharje, 73,
Connauseeteeskee, 62.
Connehana, 39,
Connelukahee, 58, 59,
Connesutah, 67,
Connor, 9,
Conososka, 39,

Consalatah, 56,
Conseehah, 67,
Coody, 67, 83,
CooeSeoo, 2,
Cooesster, 68,
Coohuitah, 68,
*Cook, 13, 33, 53,
*Cookson, 22,
Coolahtah, 52,
*Coon, 31,
Coononoo, 27,
Coooosta, 4,
Cooper, 29,
Cootiah, 41,
Cooyah, 40, 43,
*Cordery, 4, 70,
Corholuga, 32,
Corn Eater, 35,
*Corn Silk, 11, 12(2), 79,
*Corn Tassel,13, 18, 23, 49, 79,
Cornanustee, 73,
Cornfield, 5,
Cossalowa, 30,
Costalofty, 55,
Costanakoo, 66,
Costiah, 66,
Coston, xii,
Cotaguskee, 9,
Cotaquaskee(ey), 49, 57,
Cotecave, 5,
Coteeskah, 60,
Cottle, vi,
Coughloonee, 53,
Countryman, 41,
Cousehela, 54,
*Cow, 32, 46,
Cowalateeska, 28,
Cowanesta, 66
Coward, 79,
Cowatageeska, 74,
*Cowert, 24,
Cowey, 54,
Cowfeeder, 65,

Cowwaneta, 24,
Cponnaskeeska, 61,
Crabgraa, 77,
Crabgrass, 9, 53(2),
Craig, 10, 67,
Crawford, i, 37, 42,
*Crawler, 27,
Crazy Man, 27,
Crickett, 54,
Crier, 63,
*Crittenden(on), vii(2), xii, 29, 36, 37, 44, 53, 54, 69, 76, 77, 82(2), 83,
*Cropgrass, 49,
Cropper, 57,
Cross cut saw, 55,
*Crow, 15, 34, 41,
Crown, 26,
*Crutchfield, 21, 52,
*Crying Snake, 77,
*Crying Wolf, 76,
Crying Woman, 71,
Cueeste, 82,
Cuistye, 25,
Cularksaw, 63,
Culchusta, 75,
Cullacholata, 57,
Cullahsagesee, 74,
Cullalohee, 73,
Cullyer, 37,
Culquolosker, 27,
Culquotake, 60,
Culsawwee, 66
Culseegeesku, 78,
Culsowa, 22,
Culsowwee, 57, 60,
*Culsti, 14, 48,
Culstiah, 68,
Culsutee, 61,
Culsuttahee, 58, 59, 60,
Cultaclanah, 56,
*Cumberland, 77,
Cunnanatuska, 58, 59,
Cunning Witch, 57,

Cunseena, 42.
Cunseenee, 47,
Cuntaka, 47,
Cuntakee, 71,
Currey, iii, v(2), vii,
Cussowee, 70,
Cut Throat, 55,
Cuts by, 55,
Cutsuttahee, 59,
Cuttank, 64,
Cuttee, 64,
Cuttiaah, 58, 59,
Cuttiee, 57,
Dahunaula, 76,
Daldridge, 78,
Dameron, 41,
*Daniel, v, 32(6), 33, 51, 58, 70,
Darkey, 61, 66,
Darmerburg, vi,
Darney, 43,
*Dave, 40, 59,
*David, 80,
*Davis, ix, 3, 9, 11, 30, 51, 58, 64, 71, 80(3),
Davy, 34,
Dawning, 68,
Dawson, vii,
Deaf, 1,
Deaf Man, 40,
Dedaper, 9,
Deed, 45,
*Deer Head, 7, 26(2), 34, 79,
*Deer in the Water, 41, 53,
*Deer, Out of the Water, 63,
*Dennis, 24, 50,
Denton, vi, x,
DeRussy, xii,
*Dew, 7, 16,
Dhewheluhee, 54,
*Dick, 4, 8, 9, 35, 36, 46, 68,
Dickeski, 31, 32,
Dickey, 61,
*Dinah, 33,
Dirt Litter, 13, 27,

Dirt Thrower, 41,
Dirty Belly, 41,
Diver, 22,
Dobb, 36,
*Dobbins, 38,
Dog Wood, 25,
Doherty, 23, 47(2),
*Dollar, 3, 22, 31, 80,
Dorcas, 15, 30, 31, 76,
Dorhorty, 2(3),
Dorser, 38,
*Doublehead, 37, 42, 51, 52, 82,
Dougherty, 5, 30(2), 69,
*Downing, x, 7, 8, 9(2), 21, 22, 24, 28, 29(2), 30(3), 33(3), 36(2), 37, 38, 39, 46, 49, 65(2), 66(3), 76, 77, 79, 80, 82
Dragging Canee, 81,
Drawing Knife, 8,
*Dreadful Water(s), 33, 45, 68,
Drew, ix,
*Drowning Bear, 6, 24, 30, 42, 46, 50, 77(2), 83,
Drumgool, 12,
*Drumgould, 53,
*Dry, 48, 70,
Dry Skul, 2, 3,
*Dryer, 7,
*Dryhead, 44,
*Duck, 21, 36, 39, 61, 79,
Dujesta, 32,
*Duncan, 16, 71, 83,
Dunkin, 8,
Dutch, 50,
*Eagle, 11, 15, 37, 67,
Eahma, 48,
Ear Bob, 12,
Easley, vi,
Eater, 76,
Eave Dropper, 36,
Echacha, 65,
Echawcha, 32,
Echieleher, 49,
*Ecooa(h), 14, 62,

Edwards, 78,
Eentie, 4, 26,
Egaculla, 61,
Egg, 22,
Eiffert, vi,
Eight Killer, 50,
*Eldridge, 51,
Eleanor, 71,
Eleck, 16,
Eleconake, 55,
Elijah, 68,
*Elk, 40,
Ellack, 80,
Ellage, 48,
Ellick, 67,
Elliott, 15, 41, 81(4)
Ellis, 35, 49,
*Elly, 18,
*Elowee, 63,
Elwee, 78,
Enatauna, 53,
Enequah, 60,
Enetah, 55,
*England, 65, 72,
English Jim, 69,
English, 2, 8,
English George, 58,
Enolee, 60,
Equillah, 72,
Equitcha, 60,
Eskalo, 51,
Eskawat, 45,
Ess, 65,
Estaconna, 10,
Estoeagee, 66,
Esuttee, 63,
Etanteeska, 16,
Eutaeh, 6,
Everitt, xi,
Eyahtahyah, 10,
Eyawyouska, 23,
Fallen(in), 4, 17, 19(2),
Faller, 17,

Farley, 27,
Faught, 19,
Fawling, 19,.
*Fawn, 12(2),
Fealin, 15,
Feasant, 28,
*Feather, 19, 22, 23, 28,
Feeskeeska, 25,
*Fence Maker, 54, 64,
Few, 33,
*Field(s), v, vii, viii, 3, 10, 11, 12(2), 20, 41(3), 46, 48(3), 51(8), 53(2), 71, 76, 78, 80, 82,
*Fire, 43, 63,
Fire Killer, 4, 12, 17, 28, 45,
Fire Turkey, 43,
*Fish, 14, 25, 32, 45, 78, 81,
*Fisher, 22,
*Fishing Hawk, 13, 17, 31, 62,
Fisk, 22,
Flapper, 7, 30,
Flat Face, 64,
Flat Head, 8,
Flea, 42, 50,
Flint, 41,
Flure, 70,
*Flute, 58, 59,
*Fly, 3,
*Fodder, 47,
Fog, 8,
Foialeesa, 24,
Folger, vi,
Fooenoee, 15,
*Fool, 38,
Fool Peter, 76,
Foonanuler, 50,
*Foreman, vii(3), viii, 11(2), 17, 19, 50(2), 52(3), 82, 83(2)
*Foster, 5(2), 8, 48(3), 69,
*Four Killer, 54,
Fourman, 20,
*Fox, 44,
Fox Fire, 29,

Freeman, 65,
Frichancy, 49,
*Frog, 23, 25,
Frost, 37,
*Fry, 25,
Fuchalukah, 83,
Funi, 14,
Gahdo Yah, 76,
Gahtuskee, 9,
Gaither, vii,
Galoskaloya, 40,
*Gann, 13,
Garcia, 38,
*Gardenhire, 52,
Gardner, 8,
Garrett, vi,
Gauge, 23,
Gayahnah, 52,
*George, 3, 7, 9, 18, 29, 34, 37, 54, 55(2), 59, 65, 68, 76, 80,
Gessen, 62,
Get About, 82,
Gibson, 62,
Gifford, vii,
*Gilbreath, 12,
*Gillispie, vii, 7,
Ginney, 57,
Ginuey, 73,
Girl Catcher, 9,
Girl Killer, 38,
*Glass, 18, 65,
*Glory, 8(2),
Glue, 51,
Goddard, 44, 53,
Going Snake, 53(2),
*Going Wolf, 58, 59,
*Goins, 51,
Gold, 15,
Goluchee, 38,
Good, 4, 34,
Good Money, 41,
Gooden, 50,
Goose, 55,

Goss, 11,
*Gourd, 21, 51, 79,
Gourd Waters, 45,
*Grape, 15,
*Grass, 72(3), 81,
*Grasshopper, 8, 14, 17, 36, 38, 56,
*Graves, 13, 46(2), 80,
Greasy, 24,
*Green, 14, 33, 64, 83,
Green Leaf, 54,
*Griffin, ix, 1(3), 46, 47, 70, 76, 80,
*Grimmett, 25, 43, 71,
Grits, 28,
*Gritts(es), 9, 39, 71,
Ground, 10, 38, 39,
Ground Hog, 79,
*Ground Squirrel, 45,
Grubb, 70,
*Guess, ix, 14, 81(2),
Gundagee, 4,
Gunder, 2,
Gunpile, 26(2),
*Gunter, 1, 2, 76(2),
*Guts, 12, 15,
Guttee, 10,
*Hair, x, 53,
Hairy Jaw, 2,
Half-blood, 13,
*Half-breed, 42,
Halfacre, 70,
Halin, 49,
Halk, 3,
Halla, 66,
Hallowing Frog, 18,
*Hammer, 9, 41,
*Hammond, 32,
*Hanks, xii, 82,
Happy Jack, 42,
*Hard, 18,
*Hare, iv, 48,
Hargrove, vii,
Harlan(in), v, vii, ix, 8, 11, 17, 24, 52, 67,
Harnidge, 32(2),

*Harris, 1, 4(2), 10, 16(2), 29, 50,
Harvey, 58, 59,
Haskins, 56
Hatcher, 3,
Hatchet, 39,
Hawee, 8,
*Hawk(s), 18, 32, 40, 41, 57,
*Hawkins, 13, 56, 57, 78, 79,
Hayner, 45,
Haynes, iv,
Haytayteska, 7,
Head Toter, 27,
*Head Thrower, 29,
Heanna, 50,
Heeyaunah, 4,
Heflip, 19,
Hellums, 78,
Helterbrand(Hilderbrand), 13, 21(5), 25(2), 26, 49,
*Hemp, 39,
Hemphill, iii,
Hempstead, v,
*Hendricks, 35, 36,
*Henry, 1, 44,
*Henson, 78,
Hernett, 43,
Hesse, 60,
Hetzell, vii,
Heuntilaguska, 2,
Heuntologeeska, 27,
Hickkitowa, 31,
*Hicks, viii(4), ix, 13, 29, 51, 70, 76, 82,
High Walker, 45,
Hill, 69,
Hillin, 81,
Hindman, v(2),
Hix, 24,
Hodsden, vi,
*Hoe, 14,
Hog Bite, 63(2),
*Hog Shooter, 54, 68,
*Hog(g), 6, 19, 33, 40, 41, 58, 78,

Holmes, 44,
Holt, 68,
Hommany, 45,
Hood, 65,
Hook, vi, xi,
Hopkins, 52,
Hopping Dick, 72,
*Horn, 23, 68(3),
*Hornet, 54,
*Horse Fly, 16, 74,
Houghcherkeeskee, 11,
House, 14,
Houston, 27,
Howel, 49,
*Howling Wolf, 5, 27, 53,
*Huckleberry, 83,
Hudson, 43,
*Hughs(es), 16(2), 41, 71, 76, 80,
Hukleberry, 77,
*Humming Bird, 4,
*Hungry, 21,
Hungry Man, 2,
*Hunt, 3,
*Hunter, vi, 26, 32, 49, 76,
Huss, ix, 24, 71,
Hutchins, iii,
Hyatt, 81,
Hyawqua, 8,
Hyneant, 27,
Iheta, 73,
Illinoika, 34,
*Inlow, 54,
Inquah, 58, 59,
*Israel, 7,
*Jack, 9, 12, 33, 50, 54,
*Jackson, iii, 26, 36, 57,
Jailer, 37,
*Jake, 55, 62, 74, 78,
Jakewelake, 59,
Jaloiika, 23,
James, 69,
Jarnigan, vii,
Jarrett, iii,

*Jeffrey, 3(2),
Jehualee, 57,
Jekah, 58, 59,
*Jesse, 33, 62, 80,
Jewker, 8,
Jewnahaka, 48,
*Jim, 6, 61,
*Jinny(ey), 31, 40, 61, 65, 70, 78, 81,
John Ben, 63,
*John, 6, 11, 16, 17, 20, 43, 60, 68(2), 71,
Johnawanir, 6,
*Johnson, x, 21, 22, 37, 49, 54, 55, 67,
*Johnston, 59,
Johny, 23,
*Jones, viii, 45, 53, 57, 72,
Josawattah, 65,
Joshua, 36,
*Josiah, 14,
JoSkuntake, 53,
*Jug(g), 6, 33, 56,
Juggy, 74,
*July, 19, 61,
*Jumper, 22
Junaluska, 58, 59,
Junebug, 16,
Juquah, 64,
*Justice, 14, 23, 24, 44, 67(2),
Kaantusulla, 9,
Kaateekh, 29,
Kacyoha, 33,
Kade, 2,
Kaeetza, 46,
Kager, 10,
Kagg, 67,
Kahhena, 76,
Kala, 34,
Kalarchee, 17,
Kalarksa, 1,
Kalkeener, 72,
Kalloway, 23,
Kalogolaqua, 18,
Kalota, 23,
Kalovahuska, 6,

Kaneeca, 53,
Kanesa, 56,
Kankaleeska, 29,
Kannontooe, 19
Kansutotee, 18,
Kanutza, 26,
Karlascher, 16,
Karsalta, 29,
Karsawnak, 21,
Kartoo, 27,
Kartoquilla, 28,
Katchee, 77,
Kateekah, 29,
Katuskee, 54,
Katy, 54, 61, 81,
Kawcha, 46,
Kayhina, 51,
Kayooky, 71,
Keaner, 65,
Kechuaga, 36,
Keehauaga, 36,
Keelin, 15,
Keelistoga, 75,
Keellaoosta, 72,
Keenanetah, 72,
Keeneeteehee, 75,
*Keener, 68, 72,
Keenhtetee, 74,
Keeskunter, 5,
Kehena, 1,
*Kell, ix, 43, 56, 68,
Kelley, vi,
*Kenah, 65,
Kenalwheele, 38,
Kennedy, iii, vi,
Kenner, 27,
Kenoskeesha, 38,
Keowanna, 61,
*Ketcher, 26, 44, 81,
Ketchum, 12, 14, 70, 78,
Ketiah, 68,
Keucha, 60,
Keuchee, 56,

*Kianna, 55,
Kikatee, 14,
Kikotokee, 28,
Kilby, 34,
Kill Deer, 75(2),
Killa, 31(2), 51,
*Killer, 10,13, 32(2), 33, 36, 81,
Kilsewee, 79,
Kincannon, iv, v,
*King Fisher, 36, 37(2),
King, i, 39,
*Kirkpatrick, 12,
Kishikon, 32,
Kitajeeska, 66(2),
Kitchum, 79(3),
Kiuka, 70,
Knight Killer, 22,
Knockerman, 35,
Kogah, 60,
Koner, 28,
Koniskooa, 13,
Konorteski, 36,
Kooaloska, 4,
Kooeskooe, 46,
Kooka, 1,
Koonetoo, 21,
Koosescooe, 33,
Kootaha, 71,
Kotiah, 80,
Kowee, 52,
Kuikolosskee, 17,
Kukaleeskee, 52,
Kulinaka, 34
Kulksan, 62,
Kullalutta, 36,
Kulste, 51,
Kunchawlee, 1,
Kuncheescuneesjer, 1,
Kuncheestaneeska, 29,
Kunsena, 4,
Kustia, 8,
Lacy(ey), 70, 73,
Laddell, vii,

Lame Davy, 20,
Lanair, v,
Landrum, 77, 79(2),
Lang, 18(2),
Langley, 23, 67,
Largess, 15,
*Lassley(ly), viii, x, 26(2), 41, 49, 52,
Lauderdale, v,
*Laugh at Mush, 77,
*Laughing Girl, 34(2),
Lawlan, 74,
Leach, 13, 53,
*Leaf, 20(2), 35, 43, 78, 80, 82,
LeCowee, 27,
*Lee(a), 13(2), 16, 24(3),
Leecher, 31(2),
Leecowee, 68,
Lequah, 40,
Levett, 3,
Lewaga, 54,
Lewin, 62,
Lewis, x, xiii,
Liddell, iii, iv,
Lide, vi,
Liga, 72,
Lige, 55, 64,
Lightning Bug, 45, 54,
Lillybridge, vi,
Linch, 76(2),
Linder, 25,
Linkakoo, 58,
Little, 8, 18, 20, 21, 27, 39,
Little Archey, 76,
Little Bear, 8,
*Little Betsey, 65,
*Little Bird, 40, 45,
*Little Deer, 57, 62,
Little Doctor, 48,
*Little Drowningbear, 48,
Little George, 62,
Little Jenny, 49,
Little Jim, 41, 66,
*Little John, 57,

Little Mannia, 63,
Little Nanny, 72,
Little Nelly, 52(2),
Little Sally, 76(2),
Little Smoke, 56,
*Little Turtle, 70
Little Will, 57, 62,
*Liver, 14,
*Lizard(zz), 20, 24(2), 45, 47, 72,
Lizzy, 80,
Lockina, 77,
*Locust, 56, 57, 58, 59,
Loen, 62,
Lofty, 59,
Long Will, 67,
Long, 15, 18, 19,
Long Charles, 54,
Long Nancy, 42,
Long Shell Turtle, 53,
Long Will, 67,
Longfrost, 10,
Loury, 44,
*Love, iv, vii, 37, 56, 81,
Lovell, 3,
Lovely, 11,
*Lovet, 2,
Lowen, 62,
*Lowray (ry), 19, 23(2), 24(2), 44, 69, 79,
Lowze, 27,
Lubelanaess, 28,
Lucy, 21, 28, 58, 79,
Lugeesky, 34,
Luka, 73,
Lumpkin, iii,
Luwaga, 54(2),
Luwaja, 54,
Lydia, 41, 67, 70,
*Lying Fish, 16, 72,
*Lynch, 10,
Maahchee, 52,
Mackintosh, 23,
Madison, 68,
Makee, 10,

Manning, 2, 50,
Manstriker, 46, 77,
*Marsh, 52,
*Martin, 10, 21, 24, 28, 32, 77, 78,
Massey, iv(2), v,
Mastin. 78,
Maul Head, 74,
Maw, 46,
*Mayfield, 17,
Mayo, vii,
*Mays, iv, 10,
*McAlexander, 18,
McAman, 12,
McBridge, 52,
McCallie, vii,
McClure, 68,
*McCoy, viii, xi, xii, 11, 16, 24, 76(2),
McCrary, vi, 20,
McCulley, v,
McCullough, 70,
McCurty, 69,
*McDaniel, 47(3), 70, 78, 79, 82,
McDonald, 13, 76(2),
McFier, 10,
McGhee, 82,
McGuire, vii,
*McIntosh, 23, 78,
McKay, iv, 12,
*McLain, 19,
*McLaughlan, 49,
*McLemore, 15,
McMillan, iv,
McMusnon, 21,
*McNair, 19, 23,
*McPhearson, 44,
McPherson, ix, 19(2), 45, 68, 69, 70,
McTear, 41,
McTier, 10,
*Mealy Mouth, 79,
Mean Dog, 8,
Meigs, xiii,
*Melton, 2,
Merrill, 4,

Mickochee, 65,
Mihair, 21,
Mika, 24,
*Miller, 13(2), 16, 18, 19, 44(2), 67(2), 68, 78, 79(2),
Milligan, vi,
Mills, 10, 12, 29, 79,
*Mink, 2, 58,
Minus, xi(5),
Mockasin, 40,
*Mole 29, 36,
*Molly, 4,
Monkey, 2,
Montgomery, 36,
*Moore, iv, x, 9(3), 10, 14, 45, 79,
*Morris, ix, 51, 57,
*Mose(s), 15, 20, 64, 70,
Mosey, 25,
Mosquito, 38,
*Mouse, 64(2),
*Mulky(ey), 25, 50,
Mullay, iii, vii,
Munroe, 5,
*Murphy, 5(2), 21, 47(3), 49, 53, 54, 77, 78, 79, 80,
*Murrell, 18,
*Mush, 52, 79(2),
Mush Ice, 74,
Mushroom, 28,
*Muskrat, 18, 64, 65, 67(4), 72,
Nafir, 1,
Nahanah, 65,
Naheeah, 61,
Nahlahustee, 43,
Nakah, 60,
Nake, 57,
Naked Man, 39,.
*Nakee(ey), 64(3),
Namasuee, 4,
Nameconaha, 57,
*Nan, 47,
*Nana, 71,
Nance, 28,

*Nancy, 68, 69(2), 70, 71, 72, 76(2), 78, 82,
*Nanny, 6, 15, 19, 22, 40, 44(2), 46, 48, 60(2), 61, 64(2), 66, 67, 79,
Nantawogo, 27,
Naqueesah, 63,
Narcheah, 15,
Nat, 37,
Natowee, 6,
Naugkaleeska, 61,
*Nave, 41, 46,
Nawcheeah, 38,
Nayahootagee, 15,
Nayne, 28,
*Neal, 4,
*Ned, 40, 55,
Nedkinarsheeshee, 4,
Neeleka, 27,
Negoodahye, 78,
Negro Leg, 35,
Neisa, 70,
Nelika, 71,
*Nelly, 14(2), 16, 31, 41, 46, 49, 62, 81, 82,
*Nelowa, 34,
*Nelson, 2,
Netherland, vi,
Netowa, 31,
Nevins, 51,
*Nicholson, 1, 13, 41,
Nickate, 14,
*Nickatie, 63,
Nickatill, 75,
Nickochee, 66,
*Nickojack, 65,
Nickotoy, 57,
Night Killer, 80,
*Nitts, 10, 76,
Noisy, 16,
Noisy Waters, 82,
Nonatlah, 60
Nonnatla, 35,
Nooata, 28,
Noocheewee, 24,
Noonatalawyah, 59,

*Noonday, 70,
Noone Day, 19,
*North, 19(2),
*Nose, 49,
Nose Cutter, 1
Notowakee, 40,
Nowaltah, 63,
Noyeka, 50,
Oakshenantee, 40,
Oan Kah, 75,
Oastoanah, 77,
Oatacough, 77,
Oatie, 77,
Obediah, 57,
Oelonehsteska, 22,
Oesuttee, 65,
Olasaught, 37,
Old Wolf, 40,
Old Nancy, 43,
Old Tough, 40,
*Old, 27, 33, 42,
Old Bark, 54,
Old Coon, 59,
*Old Fields, 50, 69,
*Old Hoe, 74,
*Old Horse, 75,
Old Otter, 76,
Old Trout, 63,
Old Woman, 75,
Olehunloice, 16,
Oleta, 57,
Olitee, 63,
Olive, 71,
Olleka, 40,
Ollika, 57,
Olly, 4,
One Eyed Jenney, 40,
Onion in the pot, 25,
Onneelowhee, 59,
Ooacheesta, 64,
Ooahwasetee, 72,
Ooalosku, 2,
Oocahewa, 73,

100

Oochala, 34,
Oochalatah, 65,
Oochaleetah, 59,
Oochanhattah, 72,
Oochasa, 46,
Oochastasah, 60,
Oochella, 62,
Ooclahnotah, 74,
Ooclauotah, 60,.
Oocoosa, 2,
Oohaloga, 64,
Oohmemeitooyee, 42,
Oohstoooah, 24,
Oohullacha, 74,
Ookahunta 19,
Ookahyahtah, 72,
Ookanegee, 5,
Ookasata, 44,
Ookasquata, 73,
Ookatona, 37,
Ookeelah, 61,
Oolaay, 58,
Oolahnahee, 65,
Oolahoota, 53,
Oolaner, 31,
Ooleesawlee, 28,
Ooloocha, 38,
Ooloochy, 45,
Oolootsa, 43,
Oolootsa, 82,
Oolotoo, 4,
Oolsatargeesa, 27,
Oolscuntnery, 36,
Oolscuntney, 38,
Ooltaheka, 5,
*Oonanutee, 61,
Oonaseeka, 61,
Ooncheestanelah, 59,
Ooncheestanelah, 58,
Oonenakerterker, 16,
Oorah, 63,
Oosalilla, 1,
Oosaway, 47,

Oosherlohhee, 11,
*Oosowwee, 77,
Oostenakee, 62,
Oostutley, 72,
Oosulta, 3,
Ootagusta, 73,
Ootaheeta, 21,
Ootahiewtahguah, 14,
Ootalahta, 18,
Ootalla, 3,
Ootasaata, 54,
Oote(a), 46, 49,
Ootehee, 82,
Ootelah, 5,
Ooti(ie), 6, 15, 31,
Ootiah, 66,
Ootihee, 82,
Oouakahata, 3,
Oowaata, 28,
Oowahletah, 81,
Oowayaatoo, 49,
Oowayyasaltah, 66,
Ooweskooke, 14,
Ooyakee, 75,
Orchoteesta, 54,
*Ore(r), vi, ix, 23, 24(2),
Orrnah, 22,
Oskalela, 56,
Oskulska, 19
Oslasoolee, 12,
Osquinney, 64,
Ostahlanah, 11,
Ostaneunta, 45,
Osteelee, 50,
Otanneeska, 63,
Otsee, 73(2),
*Otter, 67,
*Otterlifter, 2, 17, 34, 50, 64,
Ottolahee, 59,
Oucheesah, 5,
Ougeechee, 72,
Ouletaslee, 6,
Ousawee, 7,

Overseer, 77,
Overtaken, 36,
*Overtaker, 14, 53,
Owayni, 68,
*Owens, xi, 54(2), 71, 74, 75, 82,
*Owl, 35, 53, 55,
Owoteshhe, 81,
Pach, 24,
*Pack, 82,
Packston, 7,
Paco, 75,
Page, xii(2), xiii(7),
Pain(e), 25, 26,
Palmer, 8(2),
Pan, 30,
Parber, 3,
Parch Corn, 4,
Parch Corn Flour, 58(2),
*Parks, 18,
Parris, 67, 83,
*Parrott, 3,
Parry, vi,
*Partridge, 14, 19,
Pass By, 16,
Pat, 3,
*Path Killer, 18, 26(2), 48, 51, 57, 62, 80,
*Peach Eater, 31, 32,
*Peacock, 53,
*Peak, 73,
*Pecker Wood, 50,
*Peckewood, 64,
*Peggy, 11, 35, 67, 68, 69, 71, 78, 81,
Perdu, 80,
*Perry, 17, 22, 49, 67(2),
*Persimmon, 26,
Persimmon Toater, 64,
*Peter, 73,
*Pettit, 53,
*Pheasant, 14, 17, 26, 45, 47, 52, 61, 68, 75, 76(2), 78, 80,
Phillips, 83,
*Pigeon, 18, 22(2), 34, 77, 82,
*Pigeon Lifter, 79,

*Pipe(s), 43, 53,
Pisse, 20,
Planter's Branch, xi,
Poerhowwee, 45,
Pogoleeska, 38,
Poinsett, i, ii,
Poke, 28,
Pole Cat, 25,
*Polly, 14, 33(2), 54,
*Poor Boy, 44,
*Poor Bear, 34,
*Poor, 49,
Poor Man, 37,
Possum, 21,
*Pot(ts), 13, 18, 23, 31(2), 37, 43,
Potatio, 80,
Pottit, 45,
Potts Sitting, 58, 59,
Pretty Woman, 69, 80,
*Price, 18, 23, 52,
*Pritchett, 35, 36(4),
*Proctor, 30(2), 34(3), 37, 38(2),
*Pumpkin, 1, 44,
*Pumpkin Vine, 56,
Pumpkinhop, 26,
*Punk, 75,
Purlone, 23,
Qnalquah, 19,
Quaakee, 70,
Quadahquaskee, 39,
Qualaucha, 37,
Qualauka, 2, 3,
Quallea, 28,
Quatee, 25, 68,
Quatie, 70, 78,
Quatzy, 1,
Quaua, 83,
Quessaaw, 81,
Quooloskee, 3,
Ququa, 71,
*Rabbit, 62, 66, 78, 79,
Rachael, 28,
Rackley, 79, 81,

*Ragsdale, 32(3), 34,
Rah, 22,
*Rail, 28,
*Rain Crow, 6, 10(3),
*Ralston, 41,
Ramsey, x,
Rapier, 74,
*Rat, 8,
Ratcliff, ix, 76(3),
*Ratler, 62,
*Ratley, 70,
*Ratliff, 9, 25, 26, 27(2),
Rattle Gourd, 40, 52,
Rattler, 39(2), 54, 67,
Rattlinggourd, 7, 50,
Rawlings, iv, v,
*Ray, 11,
Reagan, v,
*Red Bird, 7, 9, 13, 19, 45, 48, 82,
*Reed, 49,
*Reese(ce), viii(2), ix(2), 17, 47, 48, 52,
Reid, 69, 82,
Rey, 27,
Reynolds, xi, xii,
*Richmond, 70,
Ricketts, iv,
*Riddle, 39,
*Ridge, 9, 32, 47,
*Riley, 54, 70, 82,
Rising, 80,
*Rising Fawn, 12, 34, 35, 50, 77,
Rising Town, 33,
*Roasting Bear, 24,
Robbiet, 49,
Robert, 67, 79,
*Robin(s), 3, 17, 40, 65, 82,
*Rock, 30,
*Rogers, 5, 12, 46, 48, 53,
Rooen Wood, 69,
*Root, 25,
Roper, 74(2),
*Ross, viii, 9, 11,(3), 20, 21, 40, 49,
Rotley, 49,
Rouge, 20,
Round, 54,
Rowe, 42,
Rowena, 75,
*Rusty Belly, 33(2),
Saddlebag, 2,
Sahkenah, 56,
Sahkeyah, 21,
Sahtahkah, 58, 59,
Sahtaka, 75,
*Sakey, 70,
Sal, 52,
Salaauquee, 4,
Salawanyah, 15,
Salaxqua, 60,
Salinqua, 8,
Sall, 7,
Sallagatahee, 5,
*Sally, 8, 24, 29, 31(2), 51, 53, 64, 66, 68(2), 71, 77,
Salmon, 23,
Salola, 24, 60,
Salolaaneta, 59,
Saluwayha, 57,
*Sam, 37, 38, 69, 79,
*Sampson, 4, 33, 38,
*Sanders, 2, 8, 9(4), 13(2), 18, 20, 32, 34, 50, 68, 70, 80,
Sandrum, 21,
Sankennah, 19,
Sannacowa, 35,
Santah, 59,
Santoola, 65,
Sapsucker, 65, 69,
Saquawalta, 5,
*Sarah, 28, 35(2), 37, 58, 72,
Sarcy, 5, 17, 26, 46,
Sartake, 31,
Sartanah, 28,
Satagah, 66,
Satagatah, 72,
Satoolataney, 75,
*Satterfield, 5,

Saunders, 36(5), 81,
Sautalawock, 40,
Saweyahlase, 13,
Sawnanah, 60,
*Sawnee (ney), 4, 7, 26,
SawNee, 50,
Sawyer, 43,
Sayweenee, 20,
*Scaffold, 7,
Scales, 77,
Scalp, 20,
Sceauger, 40,
Schrivener, vii,
Scohah, 58, 59,
Scongatee, 40,
*Sconti, 30,
*Scott, 7, 8, 9, 10, 42, 54, 75,
Scousah, 75,
*Scraper, 17, 22, 25, 29, 51,
*Scudder, 47,
Scunti, 53,
*Seabolt, 51(2), 52, 53,
Secaulgah, 75,
Secowey, 39,
Section, 48,
Secunda, 20,
Seeakee, 13,
*Seed, 38, 43,
Seena, 25,
Seentahee, 43,
Segawee, 1,
Segowee, 81,
Seimpsher, 1,
Seiter, 27,
Senalla, 35,
Seneca, 29,
Sequahter, 27,
Sequanee, 16,
Sequeechy, 38,
Sequieleesa, 69,
Sesonnahee, 75,
Seteyeah, 43,
Settahnee, 73,

Setting Down, 50,
Seven, 69,
Shade, 28,
*Shadow, 6, 23,
*Sharp, 32,
Shatur, 3,
*Shavehead, 65, 72,
Shaw, iv(2),
*Shawnee John, 63, 64,
She Bat, 67,
Shepherd, 71,
Shins, 19,
Shoat, 25,
Shooboot, 76,
Shot Snow, 36,
Shot Pouch, 55,
Shulz, 49,
Shut Door, 76,
Siccowa, 32,
Sicgeeskee, 48,
Sicktowa, 6,
*Sides, 80,
Sidney, 80,
Sier, 65,
Sigcowee, 73,
Sige, 75,
Sikilley, 7,
Silversmith, 65(2),
Simblin, 45,
Simenton, xi, 4
Simonton, xii(2), xiii(2),
Sinchekiller, 55,
Sinew, 23,
*Singer, 42,
Sinka, 58,
Sisty, 34,
Sitawakee(er), 7, 8, 38,
Sitting 7(2),
*Sitting Down, 33(3), 35, 78,
Sitting Down Bear, 31,
*Sitting Bear, 39,
*Six Killer, 29, 34, 35, 42, 47, 54, 76(2)
Skaga, 69,

Skause, 7,
Skewanna, 34,
Skeyownieker, 27,
Skilla, 57,
Skilly(ey), 57, 80,
Skitata, 38,
Skitley, 80,
Skittakee, 62,
Skiugah, 69,
Skonatehi, 5,
Skouse, 25,
Skull, 22,
Skunti, 27,
Skyuke(a), 30, 39(2),
Sleaves, 32,
*Sleeping Rabbit, 52,
*Sleepy Man, 35,
*Sleeve, 31,
Small Back, 20, 36,
*Smith, iii, iv, v, vi,ix(2), xiii, 1(2), 10(2),14, 15, 28, 32, 37(2), 40, 47(2), 53, 56(3), 67, 68, 69, 82(2),
Smitt, 12,
*Smoke, 20, 21, 22(3), 24, 33, 74,
Smoke Glass, 44,
*Snail, 5, 66,
Snake House, 70,
*Snake, 5, 9(2), 11, 22, 26(2),
Snal, 71,
Snipe, 30(2),
*Soap, 31, 32, 67, 82,
Sockira, 37,
Soft Much, 55,
*Soft Shell Turtle, 43,
*Soldier, 3,
Solonakee, 12,
Sooakilla, 51,
Soon in the morning, 20,
Sore Eyed, 1,
Soulder, 26,
Souldier, 29,
Sour, 7, 20,
*Sour Mash, 79,

Sowany, 40,
*Spaniard, 49(2),
Spanish Peter, 38,
Sparks, vii,
*Spears, 21(2), 25, 75,
*Spencer, ix, 2(2),
Spikebush, 72,
Spiller, 40,
*Spirit, 10,
Spring, 5, 26(2), 32,
*Spring Frog, 43, 45, 63,
*Springston, 21, 69,
Squirl, 29,
*Squirrel, 16, 42,
Squitchee, 18,
Squluhtakee, 2,
Squonto, 19,
Squotoguska, 1,
Staff, 29,
Staffle, 44,
Stake, 48,
Staker, 11,
Stamp, 73,
*Stand, 9, 14,
Stand-up, 42,
Standbefore, 49,
Standing 5, 11, 20, 21, 25, 35,
Standing Deer, 47,
Standing Dew, 58,
*Standing Fence, 79
*Standing Turkey, 60, 66,
*Standing Wolf, 11,
*Star(r), 4, 7, 10, 25, 46(2), 76,
Starrett, iv, viii,
Staulontus, 38,
Stawanah, 66,
*Stealer, 38(2),
Steekatogah, 69,
Steele, viii,
Steeler, 8,
Steiner, ix,
Stephens, 23(2),
Steuseste, 60,

Sticcahuska, 34,
*Still, 30(2), 33(2), 35(2), 38(3),
Stinger, 33(2),
*Stinking Fish, 2, 22,
Stinson, 64,
Stone, 1, 7,
*Stool, 20,
Stoop, 31,
Stooping Deer, 23,
*Stop, 34, 47, 79, 80,
Storer, 83,
Stroller, 74, 73(2),
*Stump, 66, 73(2),
Styner, 6,
Suaata, 33,
Sucher, 8.
Suchlowga, 40,
Sugar John, 34,
Sugeeska, 34,
Suiecouhei, 6,
Sukey, 40,
Sullee, 53,
Sulsah, 76,
Sultaltataha, 75,
Sunday Fodder, 57,
*Sunday, 33, 39, 75,
Susan, 37, 73,
*Susannah, 2, 8, 21, 32, 39, 53,
Sutallah, 58, 59,
Sutleggy, 41,
Sutria, 2, 5 (2),
Sutt, 6,
Sutteah, 66,
Suttuka, 7,
Sutty, 8,
*Suwaga, 40, 63(2),
Suwaja, 66,
Suwaka, 82,
Suwannah, 58, 59,
Swan, 20, 83(2),
*Sweet Water, 6, 46, 56, 60,
Swellnees, 3,
*Swimmer, 10, 26, 31(2), 33, 77,

Swinnacauta, 33,
Switsler, 18,
Syah, 83,
Taarsta, 36,
Tacahga, 48,
Tacanty, 39,
Tackling, 37
Taconcah, 58, 59,
Taconnawassee, 62,
Taconqualoske, 56,
Tadpole, 33,
Taeskee, 12,
Tahchahsa, 75,
Tahchusa, 7,
Tahkaya, 76,
Tahkenawheelee, 35,
Tahlunteeska, 6,
Tahluntuska, 6,
Tahyahkee, 62,
Tahyana, 62,
Tail, 34, 38, 54
*Taka(h), 19, 63, 65,
Takanaeeska, 82,
Takanaseena, 43,
*Take, 45,
*Takey, 26, 81,
Talahhee, 14,
Talateska, 20,
Taleeska, 46,
Taleskee, 40,
Tallagolimtee, 54,
Tallaham, 22,
Tallasensa, 79,
Tallatoe, 15,
Taluska, 20,
Talustoeska, 19,
Tanapin, 78,
Tanchulana, 52,
Tankee, 15,
Tanner, 60,
*Tarapin, 2, 7,
Tarcheeah, 72,
*Tarcheechee, 16, 35,

Tarchersy, 43,
Targeechy, 47,
Tarkahyah, 69,
Tarkea, 3,
Tarlenetomakah, 23,
Tarlontiska, 30,
Tarpin, 15,
*Tarrapin Head, 34(2),
Tartulan, 23,
*Tassel(l), 26, 31,
Tate, 37,
Taterhair, 6(2),
*Tauney, 40,
Tauntuskey, 56,
Tawgawiskotee, 15,
Tawleescah, 63,
Tawnalsee, 74,
*Tawney, 17, 23, 38, 59, 70,
Tawwue, 26,
Tayaleese, 40,
*Taylor, 9, 12(2), 16, 17, 43, 47, 51(2), 71,
Teachary, 31,
Tecahma, 48,
Tecassanaga, 57,
Tecatoca, 54,
Tecenneskee, 62,
Techageesa, 83,
Techaweeka, 33,
Techexkah, 57,
Teckatock, 3,
Teda, 42,
Tedahquanner, 38,
Teeartoouskee, 11,
Teecama, 46,
Teechataesska, 43,
TeecooyeesKee, 41,
Teeeeskee, 44,
Teekaeeska, 46,
Teekatoska, 47,
Teeler, 25,
Teemer, 22,
Teenaneesku, 4,
Teene, 46,

*Teesasky, 43,
Teesatisha, 13,
Teesawleeskee, 62,
Teeseeska, 18,
Teesertoousky, 19,
Teeseska, 15,
TeesKee, 12,
Teeteneskee, 15,
Tegateeshe, 1,
*Tehee, 37(2), 38(2), 44,
Tekahsatagee, 15,
Tekaneeska, 28,
Teke, 6,
Tekoniska, 31,
Tekorqueona, 23,
Tekugeeska, 4,
Telakee, 52,
Telalluhee, 61,
Telasculta, 56,
Telassheeska, 43,
Teleeneenahah, 2,
Temaska, 43,
Templeton, 31,
Tenalawhista, 74,
Tenaleeska, 6,
Tenapin, 54, 55,
Tenelseena, 62,
Tenewee, 26,
Tenna, 30, 31(2), 32, 35,
Tenooa, 41,
Teolsena, 17,
Tequanny, 55,
Terhun, iv,
Termen, 22,
Terrapin Head, 81,
Terrill, 67,
Tesateeska, 24,
Tesateske, 77,
Tesateskee, 54,
Tesawheoh, 7,
Tesawhiskey, 37,
Teseeska, 6,
Teseskee, 14,

Teskegatahe, 27,
Testaonee, 10,
Tesuiska, 60,
Tesukawa, 53,
Tesuteesku, 4,
TetaKeeska, 20,
Tetakha, 18,
Tetanoskee, 20,
Tetawaw, 45,
Tetawla, 32,
Tetawlee, 1,
Tete, 39,
Tetenauska, 34,
Tetenteeska, 63,
Tetenusker, 26,
Tetonneewska, 61,
Tharp, 71,
*The Axe, 55
The Badger, 42,
The Blackbird, 36,
*The Cloud, 63,
*The Going Panther, 62,
*The Mad Woman, 63,
The Old Rabbit, 63,
The Owl, 55,
*The Panther, 81,
Theft, 20,
*Thomas, xi(2), 17, 18,
*Thompson, ix, 3(2), 10(2), 11, 16, 18, 23, 69, 81, 82,
*Thornton, 51,
*Three Killer, 42, 69,
Thulkulasker, 9,
Tianah, 72,
*Tick String, 25,
Tickakeeskah, 59,
Tickcawkeeka, 57,
Tickconnewteeswka, 61,
Tickconseska, 63,
Tickkaqnooteshha, 67,
Tickossenake, 63,
Tidwell, 68,
Tieeska, 71,

Tieeske, 74,
Tieski(ey), 31, 54,
Tiesta, 56,
*Tiger, viii, 7,
*Timberlake, 17, 46(2), 48(3), 79,
*Timpson, 9, 56,
*Timson, 32,
*Tin Cup, 4,
*Tit, 32,
Tiulsenah, 74,
To Chuck, 75,
To-morrow, 10,
*Toater, 30(3), 39,
Tobacco Pouch, 67,
*Tobacco 5, 7, 10, 29(2), 36, 38, 39,
Tocanawaska, 48,
Tocoo, 47,
Tohteecahnahkag, 41,
Toloka, 76,
Tolucha, 70,
*Tom, 12, 38, 40, 61, 65,
Tomache, 74,
Tomaka, 60,
Tomloweyowka, 13,
*Tomorrow, 77,
Tompson, 34,
Tomsilalunkee, 52,
Toniah, 65,
Tonneah, 58, 59,
Tonnoonie, 63,
Too Kor, 53,
Tooalah, 61,
Tooenonee, 48,
Tooka, 1, 3, 7, 71,
Tooker, 1,
Toolahlah, 61,
Toolough, 12,
Toona, 83,
Toonah, 81,
Toonahgee, 13,
Toonahyee, 43,
Toonanala, 51,
Toonanallah, 64,

*Toonie(i),(ey), 14, 35, 42, 57, 64(2),
Toononatatah, 74,
Toonosava, 1,
Toonoweh, 8,
Toonowwee, 3,
Toonowwee, 61,
Tooquahtah, 42,
Toosawaler, 36,
Toosawallata, 48,
Toosawallataq, 45,
Toosawaltah, 2, 75,
Toosawaltee, 4,
Toosawatte, 7,
Toostoo, 63,
Tooswalta, 42,
Tootenchettah, 64,
Tootertetah, 4,
Toothcha, 53,
Toowatah, 66,
Toowatalata, 23,
Toowttee, 64,
Tooyah, 28,
Tooyahhulla, 72,
*Toter, 22,
Toultalah, 61,
Towentaaska, 81,
*Towers, 13,
*Towie, 55,
Towney, 80, 81,
Townsend, vi,
Tread About, 3,
*Trott, 13,
Trotting Wolf, 50,
*Trunk, 7, 22,
Tsahwahagah, 79,
Tseloarahsee, 78,
Tsenahsash, 81,
Tshnweeska, 17,
Tshunaika, 10,
Tualah, 75,
Tucco, 29, 30(2),
Tuckalawsee, 26,
Tuckaneeska, 61,

Tuckasawanne, 54,
*Tucker 56, 65(2), 68, 71, 72(2), 80,
Tucksee, 80,
Tugeeeskee, 15,
Tultiee, 75,
Tuluskee, 51,
*Tumbler, 44,
Tunantuee, 27,
Tunateeska, 27,
Tunie(y), 4, 16, 26,
Tunneah, 28,
Tunnooa, 12,
Tuoonteskey, 27,
*Turkey, 13, 30, 32, 34, 37, 81,
Turkey Lifter, 41,
*Turn Over, 5,
*Turner, 1, 11, 13, 26,
*Turtle, 25, 67, 71,
Tuskageeta, 62,
Tustaree, 10,
*Tutt, 11,
Tuttiah, 65,
Tuttiee, 74,
Tutustee, 61,
Tuwaga, 83,
Tuwqueta, 70,
*Twist, 39,
Two, 1, 6, 25,
Twonegha, 20,
Twyeskee, 70,
Tyeaskey, 68,
Tyeeska, 21, 23,
Tyena, 35,
Tyeskey, 71,
Tyesska, 26,
Tying, 69,
Tynmer, 22,
Tyyeker, 29,
Tzcowechake, 37,
UcSaquah, 43,
Ueskeena, 27,
Uhaka, 49,
Ulateeska, 70,

Ullateeskee, 53,
Ulstowestee. 13,
Uluteeska, 27,
Unaketaher, 4,
Unaketehe, 50,
Uncenti, 83,
Unchawa, 50,
Uneekatakee, 19,
Unnohu, 51,
*Up the Branch, 31,
Urett, 77,
Utahtageesher, 14,
Utsak, 69,
Utseeetaee, 16,
Uwaka, 24,
Uyawgee, 1,
Uyawseeska, 25,
Van Antwerp, vii, xii(3),
Vance, 25,
Vane, 19,
*Vann, 5, 9, 10, 11, 15, 29, 31(2), 36, 47, 48, 51(2), 68, 69, 78,
Vant, 3,
Vaughn, 81,
*Vickery, 5, 30, 71,
Wacheechee, 57,
Waddee, 76,
*Wafford, 74,
Waga, 70,
*Wagon, 36,
Wagoolah, 5,
Wahatechee, 73,
Wahchetcher, 66,
Waheokilla, 46,
Wahhalah, 67,
Wahhayah, 60,
Wahhegahannah, 58, 59,
Wahheyaneka, 73,
Wahlameta, 41,
Wahlayahha, 73,
Wahlee, 77,
Wahsa, 66,
Wahseehee, 42,

Wahtoost, 74,
Wahyahaniah, 72,
Wahyahcaktoga, 62,
Wahyakakeeska, 61,
Wahyouska, 63,
Waine, 77,
Wainey, 29,
Waity(ie), 34, 62, 79,
Waive, 9,
Wakah, 64,
Wakahguatchia, 58, 59,
Wakakoo, 60,
Wakee, 67, 74,
Wakefield, 71,
*Waker, 8,
*Wakey(y), 35(3), 38, 63, 81,
Walasee, 70,
Walatooga, 21,
Walka, 15,
*Walker, v, 14, 17(2), 45, 61, 64(2), 70, 73(5), 83,
*Walking Wolf, 28, 77,
*Walking Stick, 15, 38, 43,
Walla, 57, 58,
Wallatsah, 66,
Walleah, 5,
Walletah, 77,
*Wally, 55,
Waltah, 63,
Walter(s), 5, 7,
Waltersw, 52,
Wanie, 44,
Wannakee, 83,
*War Club, 5, 57,
War Killer, 49,
Ward, 83,
Warsat, 15,
Warty, 7,
*Wash Face, 40,
*Washington, xii, 36,
Waskee, 44,
Wasp Catcher, 26,
Wassah, 64,

Wata, 34,
Watatooah, 75,
Watcheesee, 55,
Watea, 8,
*Water, 40,
Water Killer, 42,
Watermellon, 12,
*Waters, 45, 48,
*Watt(s), 3, 10, 18, 24, 29, 45,
*Wattee(ie), viii, 42(2), 63, 69(2),
Watter, 50,
Wauchusa, 16,
Wauldah, 77,
Wauscutta, 36,
Wayaneeta, 60,
*Wayne, 32(3), 54, 55(2), 58, 65,
Waynie, 61,
Weary, 79,
Weather, 37,
Weavel, 78,
*Weaver, 32,
Webb, v(2),
Weela, 29,
Weeloogah, 19,
Weelukeekee, 13,
Weever, 19,
Welah, 58, 59,
Welake, 58,
*Welch, iv, 4, 30, 57, 70, 83,
Welk, 6,
Wenenohe, 57,
Weocistah, 60,
Wessah, 61, 66,
*West, 12, 13, 50,
Whaka, 24, 27,
*Wheeler, 23,
Whip Lash, 54,
*Whirlwind, 18, 49,
White, xi, 9, 16,
White Killer, 30, 34,
*White Path, 39, 44,
*Whiteman Killer, 7, 18,
Whitfield, 2,

Wicked, 12, 30, 68(2),
*Wickliff, 56,
Wilcos, 83,
*Wilcoxson, 48,
Wild Cat, 82,
Wildcat, 45,
Wilerbrand, 20,
Wilkison, 41(2),
*Will, 15(2), 18, 26, 31, 37, 56, 67,
*Williams, xiii, 11(2), 49,
Wills, 78,
*Willy, 64,
*Wilson, iii, 6, 22(2), 26, 27, 55, 56
Wilsultalahee, 66,
*Wind, 18,
*Winn, 30, 35, 38,
Winney, 62,
Wins Blow, 24,
Wipemiass, 28,
Wisner, viii, ix,
Witch, 34, 80, 81,
Woff, 46,
Wofford, 49,
Woikket, 73,
*Wolf, ix, 19, 26, 29, 35, 37(2), 38, 39, 43(3), 63,
*Woman Holder, 56,
*Woman Killer, 50,
Wonenah, 26,
*Wood Cock, 43, 47, 52,
*Wood Lark, 35,
Woodall, 31,
Woodward(ard), x, ix, 5, 11, 12, 76,
Wool, x(2),
Wootee, 71,
Worm, 37,
Wyaluka, 16,
Wyhooska, 45,
Wyooska, 42,
Wywahsatee, 73,
Xalitowe, 13,
Yalhasalah, 39,
Yanaquah, 66,

*Yarnell, 52,
Yauyouskah, 23,
Yawayawga, 17,
Yawhee, 2,
Yeisussta, 55,
Yocisey, 70,.
Yohnawatt, 73,
Yonaguskee, 5,
Yonahneweskee, 61,
Yonawatla, 60,
Youaquah, 65,
Young Pheasant, 46,
Young, iii, iv(2), 6(2), 19, 20(2), 35, 44,
*Young Bird, 42,
*Young Chicken, 38, 72,
Young Deer, 48,
Young Dog, 43,
Young Panther, 82,
*Young Puppy, 41,
*Young Turkey, 50, 68,
*Young Wolf, 3,
Yoxah, 56,

*Surnames also enumerated on the 1835 Cherokee Census, the only known census listing citizens of the Cherokee Nation east of the Mississippi. National Archives Microfilm Publication T496, Roll 1. National Archives, Washington, DC.

www.ingramcontent.com/pod-product-compliance
Lightning Source LLC
Chambersburg PA
CBHW081134170426
43197CB00017B/2859